TRAC

NUMBER NINETY.

REMARKS ON CERTAIN PASSAGES

IN THE

THIRTY-NINE ARTICLES.

BY

JOHN HENRY NEWMAN, D.D.

WIPF & STOCK · Eugene, Oregon

Wipf and Stock Publishers
199 W 8th Ave, Suite 3
Eugene, OR 97401

Tract Number Ninety
Remarks on Certain Passages in the Thirty-Nine Articles
By Newman, John Henry
Softcover ISBN-13: 978-1-6667-3940-4
Hardcover ISBN-13: 978-1-6667-3941-1
eBook ISBN-13: 978-1-6667-3942-8
Publication date 2/14/2022
Previously published by H. B. Durand, 1865

This edition is a scanned facsimile of
the original edition published in 1865.

CONTENTS.

INTRODUCTION.

It is often urged, and sometimes felt and granted, that there are in the Articles propositions or
terms inconsistent with the Catholic faith; or, at
least, when persons do not go so far as to feel the
objection as of force, they are perplexed how best
to reply to it, or how most simply to explain the
passages on which it is made to rest. The following Tract is drawn up with the view of showing
how groundless the objection is, and further of
approximating towards the argumentative answer
to it, of which most men have an implicit appre-
hension, though they may have nothing more.
That there are real difficulties to a Catholic Christian in the ecclesiastical position of our Church at
this day, no one can deny; but the statements of
the Articles are not in the number; and it may
be right at the present moment to insist upon this.
If in any quarter it is supposed that persons who
profess to be disciples of the early Church will
silently concur with those of very opposite sentiments in furthering a relaxation of subscriptions,

which, it is imagined, are galling to both parties, though for different reasons, and that they will do this against the wish of the great body of the Church, the writer of the following pages would raise one voice, at least, in protest against any such anticipation. Even in such points as he may think the English Church deficient, never can he, without a great alteration of sentiment, be party to forcing the opinion or project of one school upon another. Religious changes, to be beneficial, should be the act of the whole body ; they are worth little if they are the mere act of a majority.* No good can come of any change which is not heart-felt, a development of feelings springing up freely and calmly within the bosom of the whole body itself. Moreover, a change in theological teaching involves either the commission or the confession of sin ; it is either the profession or renunciation of erroneous doctrine, and if it does not succeed in proving the fact of past guilt, it, *ipso facto*, implies present. In other words, every change in religion carries with it its own condemnation, which is not attended by deep repentance. Even supposing, then, that any changes in contemplation, whatever they were, were good in

---

* This is not meant to hinder acts of Catholic consent such as occurred anciently, when the Catholic body aids one portion of a particular Church against another portion.

themselves, they would cease to be good to a church, in which they were the fruits not of the quiet conviction of all, but of the agitation, or tyranny, or intrigue of a few; nurtured not in mutual love, but in strife and envying ; perfected not in humiliation and grief, but in pride, elation, and triumph. Moreover it is a very serious truth that persons and bodies who put themselves into a disadvantageous state, cannot at their pleasure extricate themselves from it. They are unworthy of it; they are in prison, and CHRIST is the keeper. There is but one way towards a real reformation,—a return to Him in heart and spirit, whose sacred truth they have betrayed; all other methods, however fair they may promise, will prove to be but shadows and failures.

On these grounds, were there no others, the present writer, for one, will be no party to the ordinary political methods by which professed reforms are carried or compassed in this day. We can do nothing well till we act " with one accord ;" we can have no accord in action till we agree together in heart ; we cannot agree without a supernatural influence ; we cannot have a supernatural influence unless we pray for it ; we cannot pray acceptably without repentance and confession. Our Church's strength would be irresistible, humanly speaking, were it but at unity with itself ; if it remains divided, part against part, we shall see the energy which was meant to subdue the world preying upon itself, according to our SAVIOUR's express assurance, that such a house "cannot stand." Till we feel this, till we seek one another as brethren, not lightly throwing aside our private opinions, which we seem to feel we have received from above, from an ill-regulated, untrue desire of unity, but returning to each other in heart, and coming together to God to do for us what we cannot do for ourselves, no change can be for the better. Till [we] are stirred up to this religious course, let the Church [our Mother] sit still; let [her children] be content to be in bondage; let [us] submit to [our] imperfections as a punishment; let [us] go on teaching [through the medium of indeterminate statements], and inconsistent precedents, and principles but partially developed. We are not better than our fathers; let us bear to be what Hammond was, or Andrews, or Hooker; let us not faint under that body of death, which they bore about in patience; nor shrink from the penalty of sins, which they inherited from the age before them.*

But these remarks are beyond our present scope,

---

* " We, thy sinful creatures," says the Service for King Charles the Martyr, " here assembled before Thee, do, in behalf of all the people of this land, humbly confess, that they were the *crying sins* of this nation, which brought down this judgment upon us," i. e, King Charles's murder.

which is merely to show that, while our Prayer
Book is acknowledged on all hands to be of Catholic origin, our Articles also, the offspring of an
uncatholic age, are, through God's good providence, to say the least, not uncatholic, and may
be subscribed by those who aim at being catholic
in heart and doctrine. In entering upon the pro-
posed examination, it is only necessary to add,
that in several places the writer has found it con-
venient to express himself in language recently
used, which he is willing altogether to make his
own. He has distinguished the passages introduced by quotation marks.

1*

§ 1.—*Holy Scripture and the Authority of the Church.*

ARTICLES VI. and XX.—" Holy Scripture containeth all things necessary to salvation; so that whatsoever is not read therein, nor may be proved thereby, is not to be required of any man, that it should be believed as an article of the Faith, or be thought requisite or necessary to salvation. . . . The Church hath [power to decree (statuendi) rites and ceremonies, and] authority in controversies of faith; and yet it is not lawful for the Church to [ordain (instituere) any thing that is contrary to God's word written, neither may it] so expound one place of Scripture, that it be repugnant to another. Wherefore, although the Church be a witness and a keeper of Holy Writ, yet [as it ought not to decree (decernere) any thing against the same, so] besides the same, ought it not to enforce (obtrudere) any thing to be believed for necessity of salvation."*

---

* The passages in brackets (all) relate to rites and ceremonies which are not here in question [From brackets marking the Second Edition, must be excepted those which occur in quotations.]

Two instruments of Christian teaching are spoken of in these Articles, Holy Scripture and the Church.

Here then we have to inquire, first, what is meant by Holy Scripture; next, what is meant by the Church; and then, what their respective offices are in teaching revealed truth, and how these are adjusted with one another in their actual exercise.

1. Now, what the Church is, will be considered below in Section 4.

2. And the Books of Holy Scripture are enumerated in the latter part of the Article, so as to preclude question. Still two points deserve notice here.

First, the Scriptures or Canonical Books are said to be those " of whose authority was never any doubt in the Church." Here it is not meant that there never was any doubt in *portions* of the Church or *particular* Churches concerning certain books, which the Article includes in the Canon; for some of them—as, for instance, the Epistle to the Hebrews and the Apocalypse—have been the subject of much doubt in the West or East, as the case may be. But the Article asserts that there has been no doubt about them in the Church Catholic; that is, at the very first time that the Catholic or whole Church had the opportunity of forming a judgment on the subject, it

pronounced in favor of the Canonical Books. The
Epistle to the Hebrews was doubted by the West,
and the Apocalypse by the East, only while those
portions of the Church investigated separately
from each other, only till they compared notes,
interchanged sentiments, and formed a united
judgment. The phrase must mean this, because,
from the nature of the case, it can mean nothing
else.

And next, be it observed, that the books which
are commonly called Apocrypha, are not asserted
in this Article to be destitute of inspiration or to
be simply human, but to be not canonical; in
other words, to differ from Canonical Scripture,
specially in this respect, viz., that they are not
adducible in proof of doctrine.   " The other books
(as Hierome saith) the Church doth read for example of life and instruction of manners, but yet
doth not apply them to *establish any doctrine*."
That this is the limit to which our disparagement
of them extends, is plain, not only because the
Article mentions nothing beyond it, but also from
the reverential manner in which the Homilies
speak of them, as shall be incidentally shown in
Section 11. [The compatibility of such reverence
with such disparagement is also shown from the
feeling towards them of St. Jerome, who is quoted
in the Article, who implies more or less their
inferiority to Canonical Scripture, yet uses them

freely and continually, as if Scripture. He distinctly names many of the books which he considers not canonical, and virtually names them all, by naming what *are* canonical. For instance, he says, speaking of Wisdom and Ecclesiasticus, " As the Church reads Judith, Tobit, and the Maccabees, without receiving them among the Canonical Scriptures, so she reads these two books for the edification of the people, not for the confirmation of the authority of ecclesiastical doctrines." (*Præf. in Libr. Salom.*) Again, " The Wisdom, as it is commonly styled, of Solomon, and the book of Jesus son of Sirach, and Judith, and Tobias, and the Shepherd, are not in the Canon." (*Præf. ad Reges.*) Such is the language of a writer who nevertheless is, to say the least, not wanting in reverence towards the book he thus disparages.]

A further question may be asked, concerning our received version of the Scriptures, whether it is in any sense imposed on us as a true comment on the original text; as the Vulgate is upon the Roman Catholics. It would appear not. It was made and authorized by royal command, which cannot be supposed to have any claim upon our interior consent. At the same time every one who reads it in the Services of the Church, does, of course, thereby imply that he considers that it contains no deadly heresy or dangerous mistake.

And about its simplicity, majesty, gravity, harmony, and venerableness, there can be but one opinion.

3. Next we come to the main point, the adjustment which this Article effects between the respective offices of the Scripture and Church; which seems to be as follows.

It is laid down that, 1. Scripture contains all necessary articles of the faith; 2. Either in its text, or by inference; 3. The Church is the keeper of Scripture; 4. And a witness of it; 5. And has authority in controversies of faith; 6. But may not expound one passage of Scripture to contradict another; 7. Nor enforce as an article of faith any point not contained in Scripture.

From this it appears, first, that the Church *expounds and enforces the faith;* for it is forbidden to expound in a particular way, or so to enforce as to obtrude; next, that it derives the faith *wholly from Scripture;* thirdly, that its office is to educe an *harmonious interpretation* of Scripture. This much the Article settles.

Two important questions, however, it does not settle, viz., whether the Church judges, first, at her *sole discretion*, next, on her *sole responsibility;* i. e., first, what the *media* are by which the Church interprets Scripture, whether by a direct divine gift, or catholic tradition, or critical exegesis of the text, or in any other way; and next, who is

to decide whether it interprets Scripture rightly
or not;—what is her method, if any; and who is
her judge, if any. In other words, not a word is
said, on the one hand, in *favor* of Scripture having no rule or method to fix interpretation by, or,
as it is commonly expressed, *being the sole rule of
faith;* nor on the other, of the *private judgment
of the individual* being the ultimate standard of
interpretation. So much has been said lately on
both these points, and indeed on the whole subject
of these two Articles, that it is unnecessary to
enlarge upon them; but since it is often supposed
to be almost a first principle of our Church, that
Scripture is " the rule of faith," it may be well,
before passing on, to make an extract from a
paper, published some years since, which shows,
by instances from our divines, that the application
of the phrase to Scripture is but of recent aaop-
tion. The other question, about the ultimate
judge of the interpretation of Scripture, shall not
be entered upon.

" We may dispense with the phrase ' Rule of
Faith,' as applied to Scripture, on the ground of
its being ambiguous; and, again, because it is
then used in a novel sense; for the ancient Church
made the Apostolic Tradition, as summed up in
the Creed, and not the Bible, the *Regula Fidei*,
or Rule. Moreover, its use as a technical phrase,
seems to be of late introduction in the Church,

that is, since the days of King William the Third. Our great divines used it without any fixed sense, sometimes for Scripture, sometimes for the whole and perfectly adjusted Christian doctrine, sometimes for the Creed; and, at the risk of being tedious, we will prove this, by quotations, that the point may be put beyond dispute.

"Ussher, after St. Austin, identifies it with the Creed;—when speaking of the Article of our Lord's Descent to Hell, he says—

"'It having here likewise been further manifested, what different opinions have been entertained by the ancient Doctors of the Church, concerning the determinate place wherein our Saviour's soul did remain during the time of the separation of it from the body, I leave it to be considered by the learned, whether any such controverted matter may fitly be brought in to *expound the Rule of Faith*, which, being common both to the great and small ones of the Church, must contain such varieties only as are generally agreed upon by the common consent of all true Christians.'—*Answer to a Jesuit*, p 362.

"Taylor speaks to the same purpose: 'Let us see with what constancy that and the following ages of the Church did adhere to the Apostles' Creed, as the sufficient and perfect *Rule of faith.*'—*Dissuasive*, part 2, i. 4, p. 470. Elsewhere he calls Scripture the Rule: 'That the Scripture is a full and sufficient *Rule* to Christians in faith and manners, a full and perfect declaration of the Will of God, is therefore certain, because we have no other.'—*Ibid.*, part 2, i. 2, p. 384. Elsewhere,

Scripture and the Creed : 'He hath, by His wise Providence, preserved the plain places of Scripture and the Apostles' Creed, in all Churches, to be the *Rule* and Measure of Faith, by which all Churches are saved.'—*Ibid.*, part 2, i. 1, p. 346. Elsewhere he identifies it with Scripture, the Creeds, and the first four Councils: 'We also [after Scripture] do believe the Apostles' Creed, the Nicene, with the additions of Constantinople, and that which is commonly called the Symbol of St. Athanasius ; and the four first General Councils, are so entirely admitted by us, that they, together with the plain words of Scripture, are made the *Rule* and Measure of judging heresies among us.'—*Ibid.*, part 1, i. p. 131.

" Laud calls the Creed, or rather the Creed with Scripture, the Rule. 'Since the Fathers make the Creed the *Rule of Faith ;* since the agreeing sense of Scripture with those Articles are the *Two Regular Precepts,* by which a divine is governed about his faith,' &c.—*Conference with Fisher,* p. 42.

" Bramhall also : ' The Scriptures and the Creed are not two different Rules of Faith, but *one and the same Rule, dilated in Scripture, contracted in the Creed.'*— *Works,* p. 402. Stillingfleet says the same (*Grounds,* i. 4. 3.) ; as does Thorndike (*De Rat. fin. Controv.,* p. 144, &c.). Elsewhere, Stillingfleet calls Scripture the Rule (*Ibid.,* i. 6. 2.) ;

as does Jackson (vol. i. p. 226). But the most
complete and decisive statement on the subject is
contained in Field's work on the Church, from
which shall follow a long extract.

" ' It remained to show,' he says, ' what is the Rule of that
judgment whereby the Church discerneth between truth and
falsehood, the faith and heresy, and to whom it properly per-
taineth to interpret those things which, touching this Rule, are
doubtful   The Rule of our Faith in general, whereby we know
it to be true, is the infinite excellency of God.   It being
presupposed in the generality that the doctrine of the Christian
Faith is of God, and containeth nothing but heavenly truth, in
the next place, we are to inquire by what Rule we are to judge
of particular things contained within the compass of it

" ' This *Rule* is, 1. The summary comprehension of such principal articles of this divine knowledge, as are the principles whence
all other things are concluded and inferred.   These are contained
in the *Creed of the Apostles*

" ' 2 All such things as every Christian is bound expressly to
believe, by the light and direction whereof he judgeth of other
things, which are not absolutely necessary so particularly to be
known.   These are rightly said to be the Rule of our Faith, because the principles of every science are the Rule whereby we
judge of the truth of all things, as being better and more generally known than any other thing, and the cause of knowing
them

' ' 3 The analogy, due proportion, and correspondence, that
one thing in this divine knowledge hath with another, so that
men cannot err in one of them without erring in another, nor
rightly understand one, but they must likewise rightly conceive
the rest.

" ' 4 Whatsoever *Books* were delivered unto us, as written by
them, to whom the first and immediate revelation of the divine
truth was made

" ' 5. Whatsoever hath been delivered by all the saints with one consent, which have left their judgment and opinion in writing

" ' 6 Whatsoever the most famous have constantly and uniformly delivered, as a matter of faith, no one contradicting, though many other ecclesiastical writers be silent, and say nothing of it

" ' 7 That which the most, and most famous in every age, constantly delivered as a matter of faith, and as received of them that went before them, in such sort that the contradictors and gainsayers were in their beginnings noted for singularity, novelty, and division, and afterwards, in process of time, if they persisted in such contradiction, charged with heresy.

" ' These three latter Rules of our Faith we admit, not because they are equal with the former, and originally in themselves contain the direction of our Faith, but because nothing can be delivered, with such and so full consent of the people of GOD, as in them is expressed , but it must need be from those first authors and founders of our Christian profession. The Romanists add unto these the decrees of Councils and determinations of Popes, making these also to be the Rules of Faith , but because we have no proof of *their* infallibility, we number them not with the rest

" ' Thus we see how many things, in several degrees and sorts, are said to be Rules of our Faith   The infinite excellency of GOD, as that whereby the truth of the heavenly doctrine is proved.   The Articles of Faith, and other verities ever expressly known in the Church as the first principles, are the Canon by which we judge of conclusions from thence inferred.   The Scripture, as containing in it all that doctrine of Faith which CHRIST the SON of GOD delivered   The uniform practice and consenting judgment of them that went before us, as a certain and undoubted explication of the things contained in the Scripture . . So, then, *we do not make Scripture the Rule of our Faith, but that other things in their kind are Rules likewise*, in such sort that *it is not safe, without respect had unto them, to judge things by the Scripture alone*,' &c —iv 14 pp 364, 365.

.

" These extracts show not only what the Anglican doctrine is, but, in particular, that the phrase
' Rule of Faith' is no symbolical expression with
us, appropriated to some one sense; certainly not
as a definition or attribute of Holy Scripture.
And it is important to insist upon this, from the
very great misconceptions to which the phrase
gives rise. Perhaps its use had better be avoided
altogether. In the sense in which it is commonly
understood at this day, Scripture, it is plain, is
not, on Anglican principles, the Rule of Faith."

§ 2.—*Justification by Faith only.*

ARTICLE XI.—" That we are justified by Faith only, is a most wholesome doctrine."

The Homilies add that Faith is the sole *means*, the sole *instrument* of justification. Now, to show briefly what such statements imply, and what they do not:

1. They do *not* imply a denial of *Baptism* as a means and an instrument of justification ; which the Homilies elsewhere affirm, as will be shown incidentally in a later section.

" The instrumental power of Faith cannot interfere with the instrumental power of Baptism ; because Faith is the sole justifier, not in contrast to *all* means and agencies whatever (for it is not surely in contrast to our LORD's merits, or GOD's mercy), but to all other *graces*. When, then, Faith is called the sole instrument, this means the sole *internal* instrument, not the sole instrument of any kind.

" There is nothing inconsistent, then, in Faith being the sole instrument of justification, and yet Baptism also the sole instrument, and that at the same time, because in distinct senses; an inward instrument in no way interfering with an outward instrument, Baptism may be the hand of the giver, and Faith the hand of the receiver."

Nor does the sole instrumentality of Faith interfere with the doctrine of *Works* being a mean also. And that it is a mean, the Homily of Alms-deeds declares in the strongest language, as will also be quoted in Section 11.

" An assent to the doctrine that Faith alone justifies, does not at all preclude the doctrine of Works justifying also. If, indeed, it were said that Works justify in *the same sense* as Faith only justifies, this would be a contradiction in terms; but Faith only may justify in one sense—Good Works in another:—and this is all that is here maintained. After all, does not CHRIST only justify? How is it that the doctrine of Faith justifying does not interfere with our LORD's being the sole Justifier? It will, of course, be replied, that our LORD is the *meritorious cause*, and Faith the *means ;* that Faith justifies in a different and subordinate sense. As, then, CHRIST justifies *in the sense* in which He justifies alone, yet Faith also justifies in its own sense; so Works, whether moral or ritual, may justify us in their own respective senses, though in the sense in which Faith justifies, it only justifies. The only question is, *What* is that sense in which Works justify, so as not to interfere with Faith only justifying? It may, indeed, turn out on inquiry, that the sense alleged will not hold, either as being unscriptural, or for any other reason; but, whether so or not, at any rate the apparent inconsistency of language should not startle persons; nor should they so promptly condemn those who, though they do not use *their* language, use St. James's. Indeed, is not this argument the very weapon of the Arians, in their warfare against the SON of GOD? They said, CHRIST is not GOD, because the FATHER is called the '*Only* GOD.'"

2. Next we have to inquire *in what sense* Faith only does justify. In a number of ways, of which here two only shall be mentioned.

First, it is the pleading or impetrating principle, or constitutes our *title* to justification; being analogous among the graces to Moses lifting up his hands on the Mount, or the Israelites eyeing the Brazen Serpent,—actions which did not merit GOD's mercy, but *asked* for it. A number of means go to effect our justification. We are justified by CHRIST alone, in that He has purchased the gift; by Faith alone, in that Faith asks for it; by Baptism alone, for Baptism conveys it; and by newness of heart alone, for newness of heart is the life of it.

And secondly, Faith, as being the beginning of perfect or justifying righteousness, is taken for what it tends towards, or ultimately will be. It is said by anticipation to be that which it promises; just as one might pay a laborer his hire before he began his work.   Faith working by love is the seed of divine graces, which in due time will be brought forth and flourish—partly in this world, fully in the next.

§ 3.— *Works before and after Justification.*

ARTICLES XII. and XIII.—" Works done before the grace of CHRIST and the inspiration of His SPIRIT [' before justification,' *title of the Article*], are not pleasant to GOD (minimè Deo grata sunt); forasmuch as they spring not of Faith in JESUS CHRIST, neither do they make man meet to receive grace, or (as the School authors say) deserve grace of congruity (merentur gratiam de congruo); yea, rather for that they are not done as GOD hath willed and commanded them to be done, we doubt not but they have the nature of sin. Albeit good works, which are the fruits of faith, and follow after justification (justificatos sequuntur), cannot put away (expiare) our sins, and endure the severity of GOD's judgment, yet are they pleasing and acceptable (grata et accepta) to GOD in CHRIST, and do spring out necessarily of a true and lively Faith."

Two sorts of works are here mentioned—works before justification, and works after; and they are most strongly contrasted with each other.

1. Works before justification, are done " before the grace of CHRIST, and the inspiration of His SPIRIT."

2

2. Works before, "do not spring of Faith in JESUS CHRIST;" works after are "the fruits of Faith."

3. Works before "have the nature of sin;" works after are "good works."

4. Works before "are not pleasant (grata) to GOD;" works after "are pleasing and acceptable (grata et accepta) to GOD."

Two propositions, mentioned in these Articles, remain, and deserve consideration: First, that works *before* justification do not make or dispose men to receive grace, or, as the School writers say, deserve grace of congruity; secondly, that works *after* "cannot put away our sins, and endure the severity of GOD's judgment."

1. As to the former statement,—to deserve *de congruo*, or of congruity, is to move the Divine regard, not from any claim upon it, but from a certain fitness or suitableness; as, for instance, it might be said that dry wood had a certain disposition or fitness towards heat which green wood had not. Now, the Article denies that works done before the grace of CHRIST, or in a mere state of nature, in this way dispose towards grace, or move GOD to grant grace. And it asserts, with or without reason (for it is a question of *historical fact*, which need not specially concern us), that certain Schoolmen maintained the affirmative.

Now, that this is what it means, is plain from the following passages of the Homilies, which in no respect have greater claims upon us than as comments upon the Articles:—

"Therefore they that teach repentance *without a lively faith* in our SAVIOUR JESUS CHRIST, do teach none other but Judas's repentance, as all the Schoolmen do, which do *only* allow these three parts of repentance,—the contrition of the heart, the confession of the mouth, and the satisfaction of the work But all these things we find in Judas's repentance, which, in outward appearance, did far exceed and pass the repentance of Peter.   . This was commonly the penance which CHRIST enjoined sinners, 'Go thy way, and sin no more,' which penance we shall never be able to fulfil *without a special grace* of Him that doth say, 'Without Me, ye can do nothing.' "—*On Repentance*, p 560.

To take a passage which is still more clear :

" As these examples are not brought in to the end that we should thereby take a boldness to sin, presuming on the mercy and goodness of GOD, but to the end that, if, through the frailness of our own flesh, and the temptation of the devil, we fall into the like sins, we should in no wise despair of the mercy and goodness of GOD even so must we beware and take heed, that we do in no wise think in our hearts, imagine, or believe *that we are able to repent aright, or to turn effectually unto the* LORD *by our own might and strength* "—*Ibid*, part 1 fin

The Article contemplates these two states,—one of justifying grace, and one of the utter destitution of grace ; and it says, that those who are in utter destitution cannot do any thing to gain justification ; and, indeed, to assert the contrary would be Pelagianism. However, there is an intermediate state, of which the Article says nothing, but which must not be forgotten, as being an actually existing one. Men are not always either in light or darkness, but are sometimes between the two; they are sometimes not in a state of Christian justification, yet not utterly deserted by God, but in a state something like that of Jews or of Heathen, turning to the thought of religion. They are not gifted with *habitual* grace, but they still are visited by divine influences, or by *actual* grace, or rather *aid;* and these influences are the first-fruits of the grace of justification going before it, are intended to lead on to it, and to be perfected in it, as twilight leads to day. And since it is a Scripture maxim, that "he that is faithful in that which is least, is faithful also in much;" and "to whosoever hath, to him shall be given;" therefore, it is quite true that works done *with* divine aid, and in faith, *before* justification, *do* dispose men to receive the grace of justification;—such were Cornelius's alms, fasting, and prayers, which led to his baptism. At the same time it must be borne in mind that, even in such cases, it is not the works themselves which make them meet, as some Schoolmen seem to have said, but the secret aid of God, vouchsafed, equally with the "grace and Spirit," which is the portion of the baptized, for the merits of CHRIST's sacrifice.

[But it may be objected, that the silence observed

in the Article about a state between that of justification and grace, and that of neither, is a proof
that there is none such. This argument, however,
would prove too much ; for in like manner there is
a silence in the Sixth Article about a *judge* of the
scripturalness of doctrine, yet a judge there must
be. And, again, few, it is supposed, would deny
that Cornelius, before the angel came to him, was
in a more hopeful state, than Simon Magus or
Felix. The difficulty then, if there be one, is
common to persons of whatever school of opinion.]

2. If works *before* justification, when done by
the influence of divine aid, gain grace, much more
do works *after* justification. They are, according
to the Article, " grata," " pleasing to God ;" and
they are accepted, " accepta ;" which means that
God rewards them, and that of course according to
their degree of excellence. At the same time, as
works before justification may nevertheless be done
under a divine influence, so works after justification are still liable to the infection of original sin ;
and, as not being perfect, " cannot expiate our
sins," or " endure the severity of God's judgment."

§ 4.—*The Visible Church.*

ARTICLE XIX.—" The visible Church of CHRIST is a congregation of faithful men (cœtus fidelium), in the which the pure Word of GOD is preached, and the Sacraments be duly ministered, according to CHRIST's ordinance, in all those things that of necessity are requisite to the same."

This is not an abstract definition of *a* Church, but a description of *the* actually existing One Holy Catholic Church diffused throughout the world ; as if it were read, " The Church is a certain society of the faithful," &c. This is evident from the mode of describing the Catholic Church familiar to all writers from the first ages down to the age of this Article. For instance, St. Clement of Alexandria says, " I mean by the Church, not a place, but the *congregation of the elect.*" Origen : " The Church, the *assembly of all the faithful.*" St. Ambrose : "*One congregation,* one Church." St. Isidore : " The Church is a *congregation of saints,* collected on a certain faith, and the best conduct of life." St. Augustin : " The Church is *the people of God* through all ages." Again : " The Church is *the multitude* which is spread over the whole earth."

St. Cyril: "When we speak of the Church, we de-
note the most holy *multitude of the pious.*" Theodoret: " The Apostle calls the Church the *assembly
of the faithful.*" Pope Gregory: " The Church,
a *multitude of the faithful* collected of both
sexes." Bede : "The Church is the *congregation
of all saints.*" Alcuin: "The Holy Catholic
Church,—in Latin, the *congregation of the faithful.*" Amalarius: "The Church is *the people*
called together by the Church's ministers." Pope
Nicolas I.: " The Church, that is, the *congregation of Catholics.*" St. Bernard: "What is the
Spouse, but *the congregation of the just?*" Peter
the Venerable: "The Church is called *a congregation,* but not of all things, not of cattle, but *men,
faithful,* good, just. Though bad among these
good, and just among the unjust, are revealed or
concealed, yet it is called a Church." Hugo Vic-
torinus: " The Holy Church, that is, *the University
of the 'faithful.'*" Arnulphus: "The Church is
called *the congregation of the faithful.*" Albertus
Magnus : "The Greek word Church means in
Latin convocation; and whereas works and call-
ings belong to rational animals, and reason in
man is inward faith, therefore it is called *the congregation of the faithful.*" Durandus : " The
Church is in one sense material, in which divers
offices are celebrated; in another spiritual, which
is the *collection of the faithful.*" Alvarus : "The

Church is the *multitude of the faithful*, or the university of Christians." Pope Pius II.: " The Church is the *multitude of the faithful* dispersed through all nations."* [And so the Reformers, in their own way; for instance, the Confession of Augsburgh: " The one Holy Church will remain forever. Now the Church of Christ properly is the congregation of the members of Christ, that is, of saints who truly believe and obey Christ; though with this congregation many bad and hypocrites are mixed in this life, till the last judgment." vii. —And the Saxon: "We say then that the visible Church in this life is an assembly of those who embrace the Gospel of Christ and rightly use the Sacraments," &c., xii.]

These illustrations of the phraseology of the Article may be multiplied in any number. And they plainly show that it is not laying down any logical definition *what* a Church is, but is describing, and, as it were, pointing, to the Catholic Church diffused throughout the world ; which, being but one, cannot possibly be mistaken, and requires no other account of it beyond this single and majestic one. The ministration of the Word and Sacraments is mentioned as a further note of it. As to the question of its limits, whether Episcopal Succession or whether intercommunion with

---

* These instances are from Launoy.

the whole be necessary to each part of it,—these are questions, most important indeed, but of detail, and are not expressly treated of in the Articles.

This view is further illustrated by the following passage from the Homily for Whitsun-Day :—

"Our SAVIOUR CHRIST, departing out of the world unto His FATHER, promised His Disciples to send down another COMFORTER, that should continue with them forever and direct them into all truth   Which thing to be faithfully and truly performed, the Scriptures do sufficiently bear witness   Neither must we think that this COMFORTER was either promised, or else given, only to the Apostles. but also to *the universal Church of* CHRIST, *dispersed through the whole world*   For, unless the HOLY GHOST had been always present, governing and preserving the Church from the beginning, it could never have suffered so many and great brunts of affliction and persecution, with so little damage and harm as it hath   And the words of CHRIST are most plain in this behalf, saying, that 'the SPIRIT of Truth should abide with them for-ever,' that 'He would be with them always (He meaneth by grace, virtue, and power) even to the world's end '

"Also in the prayer that He made to His FATHER a little before His death, He maketh intercession, not only for Himself and His Apostles, but indifferently for all them that should *believe* in Him through their words, that is, to wit, for His whole Church   Again, St. Paul saith, 'If any man have not the SPIRIT of CHRIST, the same is not His '   Also, in the words following 'We have received the Spirit of adoption, whereby we cry, Abba, Father '   Hereby, then, it is evident and plain to all men, that the HOLY GHOST was given, not only to the Apostles, but also to the *whole body of* CHRIST'S *congregation*, although not in like form and majesty as He came down at the feast of Pentecost   But now herein standeth the controversy, —whether all men do justly arrogate to themselves the HOLY GHOST, or no. The Bishops of

2*

Rome have for a long time made a sore challenge thereto, reasoning with themselves after this sort 'The HOLY GHOST,' say they, ' was promised to the Church, and never forsaketh the Church. But we are the chief heads of and the principal part of the Church, therefore, we have the HOLY GHOST forever. and whatsoever things we decree are undoubted verities and oracles of the HOLY GHOST' That ye may perceive the weakness of this argument, it is needful to teach you, first, what the true Church of CHRIST is, and then to confer the Church of Rome therewith, to discern how well they agree together   The true Church is *an universal congregation or fellowship of* GOD'S *faithful and elect people,* built upon the foundation of the Apostles and Prophets, JESUS CHRIST Himself being the head corner-stone   And it hath always three notes or marks, whereby it is known   pure and sound doctrine, the Sacraments ministered according to CHRIST'S holy institution, and the right use of ecclesiastical discipline   This description of the Church is agreeable both to the Scriptures of GOD, and also to the doctrine of the ancient Fathers, so that none may justly find fault therewith   Now, if you will compare this with the Church of Rome, not as it was in the beginning, but as it is at present, and hath been for the space of nine hundred years and odd, you shall well perceive the state thereof to be so far wide from the nature of the Church, that nothing can be more."

This passage is quoted, not for all it contains, but in that respect in which it claims attention, viz., as far as it is an illustration of the Article. It is speaking of the one Catholic Church, not of an abstract idea of a Church which may be multiplied indefinitely in fact ; and it uses the same terms of it which the Article does of " the visible Church." It says that " the true Church is an *universal* congregation or fellowship of GOD'S faithful and elect people," &c., which as closely corresponds to the *cœtus fidelium*, or " congregation of faithful men" of the Article, as the above descriptions from Fathers or Divines do. Therefore, the *cœtus fidelium* spoken of in the Article is not a definition, which kirk, or connection, or other communion may be made to fall under, but the enunciation of a fact.

§ 5.—*General Councils.*

ARTICLE XXI.—" General councils may not be gathered together without the commandment and will of princes. And when they be gathered together, forasmuch as they be an assembly of men, whereof all be not governed with the SPIRIT and Word of GOD, they may err, and sometimes have erred, in things pertaining to GOD."

That great bodies of men, of different countries, may not meet together without the sanction of their rulers is plain from the principles of civil obedience and from primitive practice. That, when met together, though Christians, they will not be all ruled by the SPIRIT or Word of GOD, is plain from our Lord's parable of the net, and from melancholy experience. That bodies of men, deficient in this respect, may err, is a self-evident truth, — *unless*, indeed, they be favored with some divine superintendence, which has to be proved before it can be admitted.

General councils then may err [*as such ;* — may err], *unless* in any case it is promised, as a matter of **express** supernatural privilege, that they shall *not* err; a case which lies beyond the scope of this Article, or at any rate beside its determination.

Such a promise, however, *does* exist, in cases when general councils are not only gathered together according to "the commandment and will of princes," but *in the name of* CHRIST, according to our Lord's promise. The Article merely contemplates the human prince, not the King of Saints. While councils are a thing of earth, their infallibility of course is not guaranteed; when they are a thing of heaven, their deliberations are overruled, and their decrees authoritative. In such cases they are *Catholic* councils; and it would seem, from passages which will be quoted in Section 11, that the Homilies recognize four, or even six, as bearing this character. Thus Catholic or Œcumenical Councils are general councils, and something more. Some general councils are Catholic, and others are not. Nay, as even Romanists grant, the same councils may be partly Catholic, partly not.

If Catholicity be thus a *quality*, found at times in general councils, rather than the *differentia* belonging to a certain class of them, it is still less surprising that the Article should be silent about it.

What those *conditions* are, which fulfil the notion of a gathering "in the name of CHRIST," in the case of a particular council, it is not necessary here to determine. Some have included among these conditions, the subsequent reception of its decrees by the universal Church; others, a ratification by the Pope.

Another of these conditions, however, the Article goes on to mention, viz., that in points necessary to salvation, a council should prove its decrees by Scripture.

· St. Gregory Nazianzen well illustrates the consistency of this Article with a belief in the infallibility of Œcumenical Councils, by his own language on the subject on different occasions.

In the following passage he anticipates the Article:—

"My mind is, if I must write the truth, to keep clear of every conference of bishops, for of conference never saw I good come, or a remedy so much as an increase of evils For there is strife and ambition, and these have the upper hand of reason "—Ep 55.

Yet, on the other hand, he speaks elsewhere of "the Holy Council, in Nicæa, and that band of chosen men whom the HOLY GHOST brought together."—Orat. 21.

§ 6.—*Purgatory, Pardons, Images, Relics, Invocation of Saints.*

ARTICLE XXII.—" The Romish doctrine concerning purgatory, pardons (de indulgentiis), worshipping (de veneratione) and adoration, as well of images as of relics, and also invocation of saints, is a fond thing (res est futilis), vainly (inaniter) invented, and grounded upon no warranty of Scripture, but rather repugnant (contradicit) to the Word of GOD."

Now the first remark that occurs on perusing this Article is, that the doctrine objected to is "the *Romish* doctrine." For instance, no one would suppose that the *Calvinistic* doctrine concerning purgatory, pardons, and image-worship, is spoken against. Not every doctrine on these matters is a fond thing, but the *Romish* doctrine. Accordingly, the *Primitive* doctrine is not condemned in it, unless, indeed, the Primitive doctrine be the Romish, which must not be supposed. Now, there *was* a primitive doctrine on all these points—how far Catholic or universal, is a further question,—but still so widely received and so respectably supported, that it may well be entertained as a matter of opinion by a theologian now; this, then, whatever be its merits, is not condemned by this Article.

This is clear without proof on the face of the matter, at least as regards pardons. Of course, the Article never meant to make light of *every* doctrine about pardons, but a certain doctrine, the Romish doctrine [as, indeed, the plural form itself shows].

And [such an understanding of the Article is supported by] some sentences in the Homily on Peril of Idolatry, in which, as far as regards relics, a *certain* "veneration" is sanctioned by its tone in speaking of them, though not, of course, the Romish veneration.

The sentences referred to run as follows :—

"In the Tripartite Ecclesiastical History, the Ninth Book, and Forty-eighth Chapter, is testified, that ' Epiphanius, being yet alive, did work miracles, and that after his death, devils, *being expelled at his grave or tomb*, did roar' Thus you see what authority St Jerome (who has just been mentioned) and that most ancient history give unto the holy and learned Bishop Epiphanius "

Again :—

"St Ambrose, in his Treatise of the Death of Theodosius the Emperor, saith, ' Helena found the Cross, and the title on it She worshipped the King, and not the wood, surely (for that is an heathenish error, and the vanity of the wicked) but she worshipped Him that hanged on the Cross, and whose Name was written on the title,' and so forth See both the godly Empress's fact, and St Ambrose's judgment at once , they thought it had been an heathenish error, and vanity of the wicked, *to have worshipped the Cross itself, which was imbrued* with our SAVIOUR CHRIST'S own precious blood."—*Peril of Idolatry*, part 2, circ. init

In these passages the writer does not positively commit himself to the miracles at Epiphanius's tomb, or the discovery of the true Cross, but he evidently wishes the hearer to think he believes in both. This he would not do, if he thought all honor paid to relics wrong.

If, then, in the judgment of the Homilies, not all doctrine concerning veneration of relics is condemned in the Article before us, but a certain toleration of them is compatible with its wording, neither is all doctrine concerning purgatory, pardons, images, and saints, condemned by the Article, but only " the Romish."

And further, by " the Romish doctrine " is not meant the Tridentine [statement], because this Article was drawn up before the decree of the Council of Trent. What is opposed is the *received doctrine* of the day, and unhappily of this day too, or the doctrine of the *Romish schools;* a conclusion which is still more clear, by considering that there are portions in the Tridentine [statements] on these subjects which the Article, far from condemning, by anticipation approves, as far as they go. For instance, the Decree of Trent enjoins concerning purgatory thus:—

" Among the uneducated vulgar let *difficult and subtle questions*, which make not for edification, and seldom contribute aught towards piety, be kept back from popular discourses. Neither let them suffer the public mention and treatment of *uncertain points*, or such as *look like falsehood*." Session 25. Again, about images :—"*Due* honor and veneration is to be paid unto them, *not that we believe that any divinity or virtue is in them*, for which they should be worshipped (colendæ), or that *we should ask any thing* of them, or that trust should be reposed in images, as formerly was done by the Gentiles, which used to place their hopes on idols."—*Ibid.*

If, then, the doctrine condemned in this Article concerning purgatory, pardons, images, relics, and saints, be not the Primitive doctrine, nor the Catholic doctrine, nor the Tridentine [statement], but the Romish *doctrina Romanensium*, let us next consider *what* in matter of fact it is. And

1. As to the doctrine of the Romanists concerning Purgatory.

Now here there *was* a primitive doctrine, whatever its merits, concerning the fire of judgment, which is a possible or a probable opinion, and is *not* condemned. That doctrine is this: that the conflagration of the world, or the flames which attend the Judge, will be an ordeal through which all men will pass ; that great saints, such

as St. Mary, will pass it unharmed; that others
will suffer loss; but none will fail under it who
are built upon the right foundation. Here is one
[purgatorian doctrine] not "Romish."

Another doctrine, purgatorian, but not Romish,
is that said to be maintained by the Greeks at
Florence, in which the cleansing, though a punishment, was but a *pœna damni*, not a *pœna
sensûs;* not a positive sensible infliction, much
less the torment of fire, but the absence of GOD's
presence. And another purgatory is that in which
the cleansing is but a progressive sanctification,
and has no pain at all.

None of these doctrines does the Article condemn; any of them may be held by the Anglo-
Catholic as a matter of private belief; not that
they are here advocated, one or other, but they
are adduced as an *illustration* of what the Article
does *not* mean, and to vindicate our Christian
liberty in a matter where the Church has not con-
fined it.

[For what the doctrine which is reprobated is,
we might refer, in the first place, to the Council
of Florence, where a decree was passed on the
subject, were not that decree almost as vague as
the Tridentine, viz., that deficiency of penance is
made up by *pœnæ purgatoriæ*.]

"Now doth St Augustine say, that those men which are cast
into prison after this life, on that condition, may in no wise be

holpen, though we would help them never so much. And why?
Because the *sentence* of GOD is *unchangeable*, and cannot be *revoked again*   Therefore, let us not deceive ourselves, thinking
that either we may help others, or others may help us, by their
good and charitable prayers in time to come. For, as the
preacher saith, ' When the tree falleth, whether it be toward the
south or toward the north, in what place soever the tree falleth,
there it lieth ' meaning thereby, that every mortal man *dieth either
in the state of salvation or damnation*, according as the words of
the Evangelist John do plainly import, saying, ' He that believeth
on the SON of GOD hath eternal life, but he that believeth not
on the SON, shall never see life, but the wrath of GOD abideth
upon him ,'—where is, then, the third place, which they call purgatory?   Or where shall our prayers help and profit the dead?
St Augustine doth only acknowledge two places after this life—
heaven and hell. As for the third place, he doth plainly deny
that there is any such to be found in all Scripture   Chrysostom
likewise is of this mind, that, unless we wash away our sins in
this present world, we shall find no comfort afterwards   And St.
Cyprian saith, that, after death, repentance and sorrow of pain
shall be without fruit, weeping also shall be in vain, and prayer
shall be to no purpose   Therefore, he counselleth all men to
make provision for themselves while they may , because, when
they are once departed out of this life, there is no place for
repentance, nor yet for satisfaction "—*Homily concerning Prayer*,
pp 282, 283

Now it [would seem] from this passage that the
Purgatory contemplated by the Homily was one
for which no one will for an instant pretend to
adduce even those Fathers who most favor Rome,
viz., one *in which our state would be changed*, in
which GOD's sentence could be reversed. " The
sentence of GOD," says the writer, " is *unchangeable*, and cannot be revoked again; there is no

place for *repentance*." On the other hand, the
Council of Trent, and Augustin and Cyprian, so
far as they express or imply any opinion approximating to that of the Council, held Purgatory to
be a place for *believers*, not unbelievers, not where
men who have lived and *died in* GOD's *wrath*
may gain pardon, but where those who have
already been pardoned in this life may be cleansed
and purified for beholding the face of GOD. The
Homily, then, and therefore the Article [as far as
the Homily may be taken to explain it], does not
speak of the Tridentine purgatory.

The mention of prayers for the dead in the
above passage, affords an additional illustration
of the limited and [relative] sense of the terms of
the Article now under consideration. For such
prayers are obviously not condemned in it in the
abstract, or in every shape, but *as offered to rescue
the lost from eternal fire*.

[Hooker, in his Sermon on Pride, gives us a
second view of the "Romish doctrine of Purgatory," from the Schoolmen. After speaking of
the *pœna damni*, he says:—

" The other punishment, which hath in it not only loss of joy,
but also sense of grief, vexation, and woe, is that whereunto they
give the name of purgatory pains, *in nothing different from those
very infernal torments which the souls of castaways, together with
damned spirits do endure*, save only in this, there is an appointed
term to the one, to the other none; but for the time they last
they are *equal*."—Vol iii. p. 798.]

Such doctrine, too, as the following may well be included in that which the Article condemns under the name of " Romish." The passage to be quoted has already appeared in these Tracts.

"In the 'Speculum Exemplorum,' it is said, that a certain priest, in an ecstasy, saw the soul of Constantius Turritanus in the eaves of his house, tormented with frosts and cold rains, and afterwards climbing up to heaven upon a shining pillar. And a certain monk saw some souls roasted upon spits like pigs, and some devils basting them with scalding lard, but a while after, they were carried to a cool place, and so proved purgatory. But Bishop Theobald, standing upon a piece of ice to cool his feet, was nearer purgatory than he was aware, and was convinced of it, when he heard a poor soul telling him, that under that ice he was tormented, and that he should be delivered, if for thirty days continual, he would say for him thirty masses And some such thing was seen by Conrade and Udalric in a pool of water; for the place of purgatory was not yet resolved on, till St. Patrick had the key of it delivered to him, which when one Nicholas borrowed of him, he saw as strange and true things there, as ever Virgil dreamed of in his purgatory, or Cicero in his dream of Scipio, or Plato in his Gorgias, or Phædo, who indeed are the surest authors to prove purgatory. But because to preach false stories was forbidden by the Council of Trent, there are yet remaining more certain arguments, even revelations made by angels, and the testimony of St Odilio himself, who heard the devil complain (and he had great reason surely) that the souls of dead men were daily snatched out of his hands. by the alms and prayers of the living, and the sister of St Damianus, being too much pleased with hearing of a piper, told her brother, that she was to be tormented for fifteen days in purgatory.

"We do not think that the wise men in the Church of Rome believed these narratives, for if they did, they were not wise, but this we know, that by such stories the people were brought into a belief of it, and having served their turn of them, the master-builders used them as false arches and centries, taking them away when the parts of the building were made firm and stable by authority "—*Jer. Taylor, Works,* vol x. pp 151, 152

Another specimen of doctrine, which no one will attempt to prove from Scripture, is the following :—

" Eastwardly, between two walls, was a vast place of purgatory fixed, and beyond it a pond to rinse souls in that had waded through purgatory, the water being salt and cold beyond comparison. Over this purgatory, St. Nicholas was the owner

" There was a mighty bridge, all beset with nails and spikes, and leading to the mount of joy, on which mount was a stately church, seemingly capable to contain all the inhabitants of the world, and into which the souls were no sooner entered, but that they forgot all their former torments

" Returning to the first Church, there they found St Michael the Archangel, and the Apostles Peter and Paul   St Michael caused all the white souls to pass through the flames, unharmed, to the mount of joy, and those that had black and white spots, St Peter led into purgatory to be purified

" In one part sate St. Paul, and the devil opposite to him with his guards, with a pair of scales between them, weighing all such souls as were all over black, when upon turning a soul, the scale turned towards St Paul, he sent it to purgatory, there to expiate its sins, when towards the devil, his crew, with great triumph, plunged it into the flaming pit . . . .

· The rustic likewise saw near the entrance of the town-hall, as it were, four streets, the first was full of innumerable furnaces and caldrons filled with flaming pitch and other liquids, and boiling of souls, whose heads were like those of black fishes in the seething liquor.   The second had its caldrons stored with snow and ice, to torment souls with horrid cold.   The third had thereof boiling sulphur and other materials, affording the worst of stinks, for the vexing of souls that had wallowed in the filth of lust. The fourth had caldrons of a most horrid salt and black water Now sinners of all sorts were alternately tormented in these caldrons."—*Purgatory proved by Miracle, by S. Johnson,* pp 8–10

[Let it be considered, then, whether on the whole the "Romish doctrine of Purgatory," which the Article condemns, and which was generally believed in the Roman Church three centuries since, as well as now, viewed in its essence, be not the doctrine, that the punishment of unrighteous Christians is temporary, not eternal, and that the purification of the righteous is a portion of the same punishment, together with the superstitions, and impostures for the sake of gain, consequent thereupon.]

2. Pardons, or Indulgences.

The history of the rise of the Reformation will interpret "the Romish doctrine concerning pardons," without going further. Burnet thus speaks on the subject :—

"In the primitive Church there were very severe rules made, obliging all that had sinned publicly (and they were afterwards applied to such as had sinned secretly) to continue for many years in a state of separation from the Sacrament, and of penance and discipline But because all such general rules admit of a great variety of circumstances, taken from men's sins, their persons, and their repentance, there was a power given to all Bishops, by the Council of Nice, to shorten the time, and to relax the severity of those Canons, and such favor as they saw cause to grant, was called *indulgence.* This was just and necessary, and was a provision without which no constitution or society can be well governed. But after the tenth century, as the Popes came to take this power in the whole extent of it into their own hands, so they found it too feeble to carry on the great designs that they grafted upon it

"They gave it high names, and called it a plenary remission, and the pardon of all sins which the world was taught to look on as a thing of a much higher nature, than the bare excusing of men from discipline and penance. Purgatory was then got to be firmly believed, and all men were strangely possessed with the terror of it. so a deliverance from purgatory, and by consequence an immediate admission into heaven, was believed to be the certain effect of it Multitudes were, by these means, engaged to go to the Holy Land, to recover it out of the hands of the Saracens afterwards they armed vast numbers against the heretics, to extirpate them they fought also all those quarrels, which their ambitious pretensions engaged them in, with emperors and other princes, by the same pay, and at last *they set it to sale* with the same impudence, and almost with the same methods, that mountebanks use in venting of their secrets

"This was so gross, even in an ignorant age, and among the ruder sort, that it gave the first rise to the Reformation· and as the progress of it was a very signal work of GOD, so it was in a great measure owing to the scandals that *this shameless practice* had given the world "

Again :—

"The virtue of indulgences is the applying the treasure of the Church upon *such terms* as Popes shall think fit to prescribe, in order to the redeeming souls from purgatory, and from all other temporal punishments, and that for such a number of years as shall be specified in the bulls, some of which have gone to thousands of years, one I have seen to ten hundred thousand and as these indulgences are sometimes granted by special tickets, like tallies struck on that treasure, so sometimes they are affixed to particular churches and altars, to particular times or days, chiefly to the year of jubilee, they are also affixed to such things as may be carried about, to Agnus Dei's, to medals, to rosaries,

3

and scapularies, they are also affixed to some prayers, the devout saying of them being a mean to procure great indulgences. The granting these is left to the Pope's discretion, who ought to distribute them as he thinks may tend most to the honor of God and the good of the Church; and he ought not to be too profuse, much less to be too scanty in dispensing them.

"This has been the received doctrine and practice of the Church of Rome since the twelfth century; and the Council of Trent, in a hurry, in its last session, did, *in very general words*, approve of the practice of the Church in this matter, and decreed that indulgences should be continued, only *they restrained some abuses*, in particular that of *selling* them."

Burnet goes on to maintain that the act of the Council was incomplete and evaded. If it be necessary to say more on the subject, let us attend to the following passage from Jeremy Taylor :—

"I might have instanced in worse matters, made by the Popes of Rome to be pious works, the condition of obtaining indulgences. Such as was the bull of Pope Julius the Second, giving indulence to him that meeting a Frenchman should kill him, and another for the killing of a Venetian. . .   . I desire this only instance may be added to it, that Pope Paul the Third, he that convened the Council of Trent, and Julius the Third, for fear, as I may suppose, the Council should forbid any more such follies, for a farewell to this game, gave an indulgence to the fraternity of the Sacrament of the Altar, or of the Blessed Body of Our LORD JESUS CHRIST, of such a vastness and unreasonable folly, that it puts us beyond the question of religion, to an inquiry whether it were not done either in perfect distraction, or, with a worse design, to make religion to be ridiculous, and to expose it to a contempt and scorn   The conditions of the indulgence are, either to visit the Church of St Hilary, Chartres, to say a 'Pater Noster' and an ' Ave Mary' every Friday, or, at most,

to be present at processions and other divine service upon 'Corpus
Christi Day.' The gift is—as many privileges, indults, exemp-
tions, liberties, immunities, plenary pardons of sins, and other
spiritual graces, as were given to the fraternity of the Image of
our SAVIOUR 'ad Sancta Sanctorum,' the fraternity of the charity
and great hospital of St James in Augusta, of St John Baptist,
of St Cosmas and Darianus; of the Florentine nation; of the
Hospital of the HOLY GHOST in Saxia; of the order of St Austin and St Champ, of the fraternities of the said city, of the
churches of our Lady 'de populo et verbo,' and all those that
were ever given to them that visited these churches, or those
which should ever be given hereafter—a pretty large gift! In
which there were so many pardons, quarter-pardons, half-pardons,
true pardons, plenary pardons, quarantines, and years of quarantines, that it is a harder thing to number them, than to purchase
them   I shall remark in these some particulars to be considered.
    "1 That a most scandalous and unchristian dissolution and death
of all ecclesiastical discipline, is consequent to the making all sin
so cheap and trivial a thing, that the horrible demerits and ex-
emplary punishment and remotion of scandal and satisfactions to
the Church, are indeed reduced to trifling and mock penances.
He that shall send a servant with a candle to attend the Holy
Sacrament, when it shall be carried to sick people, or shall go
himself; or, if he can neither go nor send, if he say a 'Pater
Noster' and an 'Ave,' he shall have a hundred years of true
pardon   This is fair and easy   But then,
    " 2. It would be considered what is meant by so many years
of pardon, and so many years of true pardon   I know of but
one natural interpretation of it, and that it can mean nothing,
but that some of the pardons are but fantastical, and not true,
and in this I find no fault, save only that it ought to have been
said, that all of them are fantastical.
    "3. It were fit we learned how to compute four thousand and
eight hundred years of quarantines, and a remission of a third
part of all their sins; for so much is given to every brother and
sister of this fraternity, upon Easter Day, and eight days after.

Now if a brother needs not thus many, it would be considered whether it did not encourage a brother or a frail sister to use all their medicine, and sin more freely, lest so great a gift become useless.

"4 And this is so much the more considerable because the gift is vast beyond all imagination The first four days in Lent they may purchase thirty-three thousand years of pardon, besides a plenary remission of all their sins over and above The first week of Lent, a hundred and three-and-thirty thousand years of pardon, besides five plenary remissions of all their sins, and two third parts besides, and the delivery of one soul out of purgatory The second week in Lent, a hundred and eight and-fifty thousand years of pardon, besides the remission of all their sins, and a third part besides, and the delivery of one soul The third week in Lent, eighty thousand years, besides a plenary remission, and the delivery of one soul out of purgatory The fourth week in Lent, threescore thousand years of pardon, besides a remission of two-thirds of all their sins, and one plenary remission, and one soul delivered. The fifth week, seventy-nine thousand years of pardon, and the deliverance of two souls, only the two thousand seven hundred years that are given for the Sunday, may be had twice that day, if they will visit the altar twice, and as many quarantines The sixth week, two hundred and five thousand years, besides quarantines and four plenary pardons Only on Palm Sunday, whose portion is twenty-five thousand years, it may be had twice that day. And all this is the price of him that shall, upon these days, visit the altar in the church of St Hilary And this runs on to the Fridays, and many festivals, and other solemn days in the other parts of the year."—*Jer. Taylor*, vol. xi. p 53–56

[The doctrine then of pardons, spoken of in the Article, is the doctrine maintained and acted on in the Roman Church, that remission of the penalties of sin in the next life may be obtained by the power of the Pope, with such abuses as money payments consequent thereupon.*]

3. Veneration and worshipping of Images and Relics.

That the Homilies do not altogether discard reverence towards relics, has already been shown. Now let us see what they do discard.

"What meaneth it that Christian men, after the use of the Gentiles idolaters *cap and kneel* before images? which, if they had any sense and gratitude, would kneel before men, carpenters, masons, plasterers, founders, and goldsmiths, their makers and framers, by whose means they have attained this honor, which else should have been evil-favored, and rude lumps of clay or plaster, pieces of timber, stone, or metal, without shape or fashion, and so without all estimation and honor, as that idol in the Pagan poet confesseth, saying, 'I was once a vile block, but now I am become a god,' &c What a fond thing is it for man, who hath life and reason, to bow himself to a dead and insensible image, the work of his own hand! Is not this stooping and kneeling before them [adoration of them], which is forbidden so earnestly by GOD's word? Let such as so fall down before images of saints, know and confess that they exhibit that honor to dead stocks and stones, which the saints themselves, Peter, Paul, and Barnabas, would not to be given to them, being alive, which the angel of GOD forbiddeth to be given to him And if they say they exhibit such honor not to the image, but to the saint whom it representeth, they are convicted of folly, to believe that they please saints with that honor, which they abhor as a spoil of GOD's honor "—*Homily on Peril of Idolatry*, p 191

---

* " The pardons then, spoken of in the Article, are large and reckless indulgences from the penalties of sin obtained on money payments."—1st ed

Again :—

"Thus far Lactantius, and much more, too long here to write, of *candle lighting* in temples *before images and idols* for religion, whereby appeareth both the foolishness thereof, and also that in opinion and act we do agree altogether in our candle-religion with the Gentiles idolaters What meaneth it that they, after the example of the Gentiles idolaters, *burn incense, offer up gold* to images. *hang up crutches*, chains, and ships, legs, arms, and whole men and women of wax, before images, as though by them, or saints (as they say) they were delivered from lameness, sickness, captivity, or shipwreck? Is not this 'colere imagines,' to worship images, so earnestly forbidden in GOD's word? If they deny it, let them read the eleventh chapter of Daniel the Prophet, who saith of Antichrist, 'He shall worship a god, whom his fathers knew not, with gold, silver, and with precious stones, and other things of pleasure ' in which place the Latin word is *colet*" .   . 'To increase this madness, wicked men, which have the keeping of such images, for their great lucre and advantage, after the example of the Gentiles idolaters, have reported and spread abroad, as well by *lying tales* as written fables, divers miracles of images ; as that such an image miraculously was sent from heaven, even like the Palladium, or Magna Diana Ephesiorum Such another was as miraculously found in the earth, as the man's head was in the Capitol, or the horse's head in Capua Such an image was brought by angels Such an one came itself far from the East to the West, as Dame Fortune fled to Rome Such an image of our Lady was painted by St Luke, whom of a physician they have made a painter for that purpose. Such an one an hundred yokes of oxen could not move, like Bona Dea, whom the ship could not carry , or Jupiter Olympus, which laughed the artificers to scorn, that went about to remove him to Rome Some images, though they were hard and stony, yet for tender heart and pity, wept. Some, like Castor and Pollux, helping their friends in battle, sweat, as marble pillars do in dankish weather Some spake more monstrously than ever did Balaam's ass, who had life and

breath in him Such a cripple came and saluted this saint of
oak, and by and by he was made whole, and, lo! here hangeth
his crutch Such an one in a tempest vowed to St Christopher,
and 'scaped, and behold, here is a ship of wax Such an one,
by St Leonard's help, brake out of prison, and see where his
fetters hang " . "The Relics we must kiss and *offer unto*,
specially on Relic Sunday And while we offer (that we should
not be weary, or repent us of our cost), the *music* and *minstrelsy*
goeth merrily all the offertory time, with praising and calling
upon those saints, whose relics be then in presence Yea, and
the water also, wherein those relics have been dipped, must with
great reverence be reserved, as very holy and effectuous." .

"Because Relics were so gainful, few places were there but they
had Relics provided for them And for more *plenty* of Relics,
some one saint had many heads, one in one place, and another in
another place Some had six arms, and twenty-six fingers And
where our LORD bare His cross alone, if all the pieces of the
relics thereof were gathered together, the greatest ship in England would scarcely bear them, and yet the greatest part of it,
they say, doth yet remain in the hands of the Infidels, for the
which they pray in their beads-bidding, that they may get it
also into their hands, for such godly use and purpose And not
only the bones of the saints, but every thing appertaining to
them, was a holy relic. In some place they offer a sword, in
some the scabbard, in some a shoe, in some a saddle that had
been set upon some holy horse, in some the coals wherewith St.
Laurence was roasted, in some place the tail of the ass which
our LORD JESUS CHRIST sat on, to be *kissed and offered unto* for a
relic. For rather than they would lack a relic, they would offer
you *a horse bone instead of a virgin s arm*, or the tail of the ass
to be kissed and offered unto for relics O wicked, impudent,
and most shameless men, the devisers of these things! O silly, ·
foolish, and dastardly daws, and more beastly than the ass whose
tail they kissed, that believe such things!" . . "Of these
things already rehearsed, it is evident that our image maintainers
have not only made images, and set them up in temples, as did

the Gentiles idolaters their idols; but also that they have had
the same idolatrous opinions of the saints, to whom they have
made images, which the Gentiles idolaters had of their false
gods, and have not only *worshipped* their images with the same
rites, ceremonies, superstitions, and all circumstances, as did the
Gentiles idolaters their idols, but in many points have also far
exceeded them in all wickedness, foolishness, and madness."—
Homily on Peril of Idolatry, pp 193–197

It will be observed that in this extract, as elsewhere in the Homilies, it is implied that the
Bishop or the Church of Rome is Antichrist;
but this is a statement bearing on prophetical
interpretation, not on doctrine; and one besides
which cannot be reasonably brought to illustrate
or explain any of the positions of the Articles;
and therefore it may be suitably passed over.

In another place the Homilies speak as follows:

" Our churches stand full of such great puppets, *wondrously
decked and adorned*, garlands and coronets be set on their heads,
precious pearls hanging about their necks, their fingers shine
with rings, set with precious stones; their dead and stiff
bodies are clothed with garments stiff with gold   You would
believe that the images of our men-saints were some princes of
Persia land with their proud apparel, and the idols of our
women-saints were *nice and well-trimmed harlots, tempting their
paramours to wantonness* whereby the saints of GOD are not
honored, but most dishonored, and their godliness, soberness,
chastity, contempt of riches, and of the vanity of the world, defaced and brought in doubt by such *monstrous decking*, most differ-
ing from their sober and godly lives.   And because the whole
pageant must thoroughly be played, it is not enough thus to deck
idols, but at last come in the priests themselves, likewise decked
with gold and pearl, that they may be meet servants for such

lords and ladies, and fit worshippers of such gods and goddesses
And with a solemn pace they pass forth before these *golden pup-*
pets and *fall down* to the ground on their marrow-bones before
these honorable idols, and then rising up again, *offer up odors and*
incense unto them, to give the people an example of double idolatry, by worshipping not only the idol, but the gold also, and
riches, wherewith it is garnished   Which thing, the most part
of our old Martyrs, rather than they would do, or once *kneel,* or
offer up one crumb of *incense* before an image, suffered most cruel
and terrible deaths, as the histories of them at large do declare "
   . " O books and scriptures, in the which the devilish
schoolmaster, Satan, hath penned the lewd lessons of wicked
idolatry, for his dastardly disciples and scholars to behold, read,
and learn, to GOD'S most high dishonor, and their most horrible
damnation !   Have we not been much bound, think you, to those
which should have taught us the truth out of GOD's Book and his
Holy Scripture, that they have shut up that Book and Scripture
from us, and none of us so bold as once to open it, or read in it ?
And instead thereof, to spread us abroad these goodly, carved,
and gilded books and painted scripture, to teach us such good and
godly lessons ?   Have not they done well, after they ceased to
stand in pulpits themselves, and to teach the people committed to
their instruction, keeping silence of God's word, and become
dumb dogs (as the Prophet calleth them), to set up in their stead,
on every pillar and corner of the church, such goodly doctors, as
dumb, but more wicked than themselves be?   We need not to
complain of the lack of one dumb parson, having so many dumb
devilish vicars (I mean these idols and painted puppets) to teach
in their stead   Now in the mean season, whilst the dumb and
dead idols stand thus *decked and clothed,* contrary to GOD's law
and commandment, the poor Christian people, the lively images
of GOD, commended to us so tenderly by our SAVIOUR CHRIST, as
most dear to Him, stand naked, shivering for cold, and their
teeth chattering in their heads, and no man covereth them, are
pined with hunger and thirst, and no man giveth them a penny
to refresh them, whereas pounds be ready at all times (contrary
   3 *

to GOD'S word and will) to *deck and trim* dead stocks and stones,
which neither feel cold, hunger, nor thirst."—*Homily on Peril of
Idolatry*, p. 219–222.

Again, with a covert allusion to the abuses of the
day, the Homilist says elsewhere, of Scripture :—

"There shall you read of Baal, Moloch, Chamos, Melchom,
Ballpeor, Astaroth, Bel, the Dragon, Priapus, the brazen Serpent,
the twelve Signs, and many others, unto whose images the people,
with great devotion, invented *pilgrimages, precious decking* and
censing them, *kneeling down* and *offering* to them, thinking that an
high merit before GOD, and to be esteemed above the precepts
and commandments of GOD "—*Homily on Good Works*, p. 42

Again, soon after :—

"What man, having any judgment or learning, joined with a
true zeal unto GOD, doth not see and lament to have entered into
CHRIST'S religion, such false doctrine, superstition, idolatry, hypocrisy, and other enormities and abuses, so as by little and little,
through the sour leaven thereof, the sweet bread of GOD'S holy
word hath been much hindered and laid apart? Never had the
Jews, in their most blindness, so many *pilgrimages* unto images,
nor used so much *kneeling, kissing,* and *censing* of them, as hath
been used in our time   Sects and feigned religions were neither
the fortieth part so many among the Jews, nor more superstitiously and ungodly abused, than of late years they have been
among us   which sects and religions had so many hypocritical
and feigned works in their state of religion, as they arrogantly
named it, that their lamps, as they said, ran always over, able to
satisfy not only for their own sins, but also for all other their
benefactors, brothers, and sisters of religion, as most ungodly and
craftily they had persuaded the multitude of ignorant people,
keeping in divers places, as it were, marts or markets of merits,
being full of their holy relics, images, shrines, and works of over-
flowing abundance, ready to be sold, and all things which they

had were called holy—holy cowls, holy girdles, holy pardons, holy beads, holy shoes, holy rules, and all full of holiness. And what thing can be more foolish, more superstitious, or ungodly, than that men, women, and children, should wear a friar's coat to deliver them from agues or pestilence, or when they die, or when they be buried, cause it to be cast upon them, *in hope thereby to be saved?* Which superstition, although (thanks be to GOD!) it hath been little used in this realm, yet in divers other realms it hath been, and yet is, used among many, both learned and unlearned "—*Homily on Good Works*, pp 45, 46.

[Once more :—

"True religion, then, and pleasing of GOD, standeth not in making, setting up, painting, gilding, clothing, and decking of dumb and dead images (which be but great puppets and babies for old fools in dotage, and wicked idolatry, to dally and play with), nor in kissing of them, capping, kneeling, offering to them, incensing of them, setting up of candles, hanging up of legs, arms, or whole bodies of wax before them, or praying or asking of them, or of saints, things belonging only to GOD to give   But all these things be vain and abominable and most damnable before GOD "—*Homily on Peril of Idolatry*, p 223]

Now the veneration and worship condemned in these and other passages are such as these : kneeling before images, lighting candles to them, offering them incense, going on pilgrimage to them, hanging up crutches, &c., before them, lying tales about them, belief in miracles as if wrought by them through illusion of the devil, decking them up immodestly, and providing incentives by them to bad passions ; and, in like manner, merry music and minstrelsy, and licentious practices in honor of relics, counterfeit relics, multiplication of them, absurd pretences about them. This is what the Article means by "the Romish doctrine," which in agreement to one of the above extracts, it calls "a fond thing," *res futilis;* for who can ever hope, except the grossest and most blinded minds, to be gaining the favor of the blessed saints, while they come with unchaste thoughts and eyes that cannot cease from sin; and to be profited by "pilgrimage-going," in which "Lady Venus and her son Cupid were rather worshipped wantonly in the flesh, than GOD the FATHER, and our SAVIOUR CHRIST HIS SON, truly worshipped in the SPIRIT?"

Here again it is remarkable that, urged by the truth of the allegation, the Council of Trent is obliged, both to confess the above-mentioned enormities in the veneration of relics and images, and to forbid them :—

> " Into these holy and salutary observances, should any abuses creep, of these the Holy Council strongly [vehementer] desires the utter extinction, so that no images of a false doctrine, and supplying to the uninstructed opportunity of perilous error, should be set up   . All superstition also in invocation of saints, veneration of relics, and sacred use of images, be put away, all *filthy lucre* be cast out of doors; and *all wantonness* be avoided; *so that images be not painted or adorned with an immodest beauty;* or the celebration of Saints and attendance on Relics *be abused to revelries and drunkennesses,* as though festival days were kept in honor of saints by *luxury and lasciviousness* "—*Sess* 25.

[On the whole, then, by the Romish doctrine of the veneration and worshipping of images and relics, the Article means all maintenance of those idolatrous honors which have been and are paid them so commonly throughout the Church of Rome, with the superstitions, profanities, and impurities consequent thereupon.]

4. Invocation of Saints.

By "invocation" here is not meant the mere circumstance of addressing beings out of sight, because we use the Psalms in our daily service, which are frequent in invocations of Angels to praise and bless GOD. In the Benedicite too we address "the spirits and souls of the righteous."

Nor is it a "fond" invocation to pray that unseen beings may bless us; for this [Bishop Ken does in his Evening Hymn:—

> "O may my guardian while I sleep,
>   Close to my bed his vigils keep,
>   His love angelical *instil*,
>   Stop all the avenues of ill," &c]*

On the other hand, judging from the example set us in the Homilies themselves, invocations are not censurable, and certainly not "fond," if we mean nothing definite by them, addressing them to beings which we *know* cannot hear, and using them as interjections. The Homilist seems to avail himself of this proviso in a passage, which

---

* [A passage here occurred in 1st edition upon Rev i 4]

will serve to begin our extracts in illustration of the *superstitious* use of invocations :—

"We have left Him neither heaven, nor earth, nor water, nor country, nor city, peace nor war to rule and govern, neither men, nor beasts, nor their diseases to cure, that a godly man might justly, for zealous indignation, cry out, *O heaven, O earth, and seas*,* what madness and wickedness against GOD are men fallen into! What dishonor do the creatures to their CREATOR and MAKER! And if we remember GOD sometimes, yet, because we doubt of His ability or will to help, we join to Him another helper, as if he were a noun adjective, using these sayings · such as learn, GOD and St Nicholas be my speed such as neese, GOD help and St John to the horse, GOD and St Loy save thee. Thus are we become like horses and mules, which have no understanding For is there not one GOD only, who by His power and wisdom made all things, and by His providence governeth the same, and by His goodness maintaineth and saveth them? Be not all things of Him, by Him, and through Him? Why dost thou *turn from the* CREATOR *to the creatures?* This is the manner of the Gentiles idolaters, but thou art a Christian, and therefore by CHRIST alone hast access to GOD the FATHER, and help of Him only "—*Homily on Peril of Idolatry*, p 189.

Again, just before—

"Terentius Varro showeth, that there were three hundred Jupiters in his time there were no fewer Veneres and Dianæ · we had no fewer Christophers, Ladies, and Mary Magdalens, and other saints Œnomaus and Hesiodus show, that in their time there were thirty thousand gods I think we had no fewer saints, to whom we gave the honor due to GOD And they have not only spoiled the true living GOD of His due honor in temples, cities, countries, and lands, by such devices and inventions as the

---

* "O cœlum, O terra, O maria Neptuni "—*Terent Adelph* , v. 3.

Gentiles idolaters have done before them, but the sea and waters have as well special saints with them, as they had gods with the Gentiles, Neptune, Triton Nereus, Castor and Pollux, Venus, and such other· in whose places become St Christopher, St Clement, and divers other, and specially our Lady, to whom shipmen sing, 'Ave maris stella' Neither hath the fire escaped their idolatrous inventions   For, instead of Vulcan and Vesta, the Gentiles' gods of the fire, our men have placed St Agatha, and make litters on her day to quench fire with   Every artificer and profession hath his special saint, as a peculiar god   As for example, scholars have St Nicholas and St Gregory, painters, St Luke; neither lack soldiers their Mars, nor lovers their Venus, amongst Christians   All diseases have their special saints, as gods the curers of them,   the falling-evil St Cornelio, the tooth-ache St. Apollin, &c   Neither do beasts nor cattle lack their gods with us, for St Loy is the horseleech, and St. Anthony the swineherd "
—*Ibid.*, p 188

The same subject is introduced in connection with a lament over the falling off of attendance on religious worship consequent upon the Reformation :—

" GOD's vengeance hath been and is daily provoked, because much wicked people pass nothing to resort to the church, either for that they are so sore blinded, that they understand nothing of GOD and godliness, and care not with devilish example to offend their neighbors, or else for that they see the Church altogether scorned of such *gay gazing sights*, as their gross fantasy was greatly delighted with, because they see the false religion abandoned, and the true restored, which seemeth an unsavory thing to their unsavory taste, as may appear by this, that a woman said to her neighbor, 'Alas, gossip, what shall we now do at church, since all the saints are taken away, since all the *goodly sights* we were wont to have are gone, since we cannot hear the like *piping, singing, chanting,* and *playing upon the organs,* that we could before?' But, dearly beloved, we ought greatly to rejoice, and give GOD thanks, that our churches are delivered of all those things which displeased GOD so sore, and *filthily defiled* His house and His place of prayer, for the which He hath justly destroyed many nations, according to the saying of St Paul · 'If any man defile the temple of GOD, GOD will him destroy' And this ought we greatly to praise GOD for, that *superstitious* and *idolatrous* manners as were utterly naught, and defaced GOD's glory, are utterly abolished, as they most justly deserved, and yet those things that either GOD was honored with, or His people edified, are decently retained, and in our churches comely practised."— *On the Place and Time of Prayer*, pp. 293, 294.

Again :—

"There are certain conditions most requisite to be found in every such a one that must be called upon, which if they be not found in Him unto whom we pray, then doth our prayer avail us nothing, but is altogether in vain

"The first is this, that He, to whom we make our prayers, be able to help us The second is, that He will help us. The third is, that He be such a one as may hear our prayers The fourth is, that He understand better than ourselves what we lack and how far we have need of help If these things be to be found in any other, saving only GOD, then may we lawfully call upon some other besides GOD But what man is so gross, but he well understandeth that these things are only proper to Him who is omnipotent, and knoweth all things, even the very secrets of the heart, that is to say, only and to GOD alone? Whereof it followeth that we must call neither upon angel, nor yet upon saint, but only and solely upon GOD, as St Paul doth write ' How shall men call upon Him, in whom they have not believed?' So that *invocation* or *prayer* may not be made without faith in Him on whom they call, but that we must first *believe* in Him before we can make our prayer unto Him, whereupon we must only and solely pray unto GOD For to say that we should *believe* in either angel or saint, or in any other living creature, were *most horrible blasphemy* against GOD and His holy word neither ought this fancy to enter into the heart of any Christian man, because we are expressly taught in the word of the LORD only to repose our faith in the blessed TRINITY, in whose only name we are also baptized, according to the express commandment of our SAVIOUR JESUS CHRIST, in the last of St Matthew

"But that the truth hereof may better appear, even to them that be most simple and unlearned, let us consider what prayer is St Augustine calleth it a lifting up of the mind to GOD, that is to say, an humble and lowly pouring out of the heart to GOD Isidorus saith, that it is an affection of the heart, and not a labor of the lips So that, by these plans, true prayer doth consist not so much in the outward sound and voice of words, as in the inward groaning and crying of the heart to GOD

"Now, then, is there any angel, any virgin, any patriarch, or prophet, among the dead, that can understand or know the meaning of the heart? The Scripture saith, 'it is GOD that searcheth the heart and reins, and that He only knoweth the hearts of the children of men' As for the saints, they have so little knowledge of the secrets of the heart, that many of the ancient Fathers greatly doubt whether they know any thing at all, that is commonly done on earth And albeit some think they do, yet St Augustine, a doctor of great authority, and also antiquity, hath his opinion of them, that they know no more what we do on earth, than we know what they do in heaven For proof whereof, he allegeth the words of Isaiah the prophet, where it is said, 'Abraham is ignorant of us, and Israel knoweth us not' His mind therefore is this, not that we should put any religion in *worshipping* them, or *praying* unto them, but that we should honor them by following their virtuous and godly life For, as he witnesseth in another place, the martyrs, and holy men in time past, were wont, after their death, to be *remembered* and *named* of the priest at divine service but never to be *invocated* or *called upon* And why so? Because the priest, saith he, is GOD's priest, and not theirs, whereby he is bound to call upon GOD, and not upon them. . . . . . . O but I dare not (will some man

say) trouble God at all times with my prayers : we see that in
king's houses, and courts of princes, men cannot be admitted,
unless they first use the help and means of some special noble-
man, to come to the speech of the king, and to obtain the thing
that they would have

"CHRIST, sitting in heaven, hath an everlasting priesthood, and
always prayeth to His FATHER for them that be penitent, obtaining, by virtue of His wounds, which are evermore in the sight of
God, not only perfect remission of our sins, but also all other necessaries that we lack in this world , so that this Holy Mediator
is sufficient in heaven, and needeth no others to help Him.

" Invocation is a thing *proper unto* God, which if we attribute
unto the saints, it soundeth unto their reproach, neither can they
well bear it at our hands   When Paul healed a certain lame man,
which was impotent in his feet, at Lystra, the people would have
done sacrifice unto him and Barnabas , who, rending their clothes,
refused it, and exhorted them to *worship* the true God   Likewise
in the Revelation, when St John *fell before the angel's feet to worship him*, the angel would not permit him to do it, but commanded
him that he should worship God   Which examples declare unto
us, that the saints and angels in heaven will not have us to do
any honor unto them, *that is due and proper unto* God "—*Homily
on Prayer*, p 272–277

Whereas, then, it has already been shown that
not *all* invocation is wrong, this last passage plainly tells us *what kind* of invocation is not allowable, or what is meant by invocation in its excep-
tionable sense : viz., " a thing proper to God," as
being part of the " honor that is due and proper
unto God."   And two instances are specially
given of such calling and invocating, viz., *sacri-
ficing*, and *falling down in worship*.   Besides
this, the Homilist adds, that it is wrong to pray

to them for "necessaries in this world," and to
accompany their services with "piping, singing,
chanting, and playing" on the organ, and of in-
voking saints as patrons of particular elements,
countries, arts, or remedies.

Here again, as before, the Article gains a witness and concurrence from the Council of Trent.
"Though," say the divines there assembled, "the
Church has been accustomed sometimes to celebrate a few masses to the honor and remembrance
of saints, yet she *doth not teach that sacrifice is
offered to them*, but to GOD alone, who crowned
them; wherefore neither is the priest wont to say,
I offer sacrifice to thee, O Peter, or O Paul, but
to GOD." (Sess. 22.)

Or, to know what is meant by fond invocations,
we may refer to the following passage of Bishop
Andrews's answer to Cardinal Perron :—

"This one point is needful to be observed throughout all the
Cardinal's answer, that he hath framed to himself five distinctions —(1) Prayer *direct*, and prayer *oblique*, or indirect   (2)
Prayer *absolute*, and prayer *relative*   (3) Prayer *sovereign*, and
prayer *subaltern*   (4) Prayer *final*, and prayer *transitory*   (5)
Prayer *sacrificial*, and prayer *out of*, or *from the sacrifice*   Prayer
direct, absolute, final, sovereign, sacrificial, that must not be made
to the saints, but to GOD only   but as for *prayer oblique, relative,
transitory, subaltern, from*, or *out of the sacrifice*, that (saith he) we
may make to the saints

"For all the world, like the question in Scotland, which was
made some fifty years since, whether the *Pater noster* might not
be said to *saints*   For then they in like sort devised the distinc-

tion of—(1.) *Ultimate, et non ultimate* (2.) *Principaliter, et minus principaliter* (3.) *Primarie, et secundarie · Capiendo stricte, et capiendo large* And as for *ultimate, principaliter, primarie, et capiendo stricte*, they concluded it must go to God, but *non ultimate, minus principaliter, secundarie, et capiendo large*, it might be allowed *saints*

"Yet it is sure, that in these distinctions is the whole substance of his answer. And whensoever he is pressed, he flees straight to his *prayer relative* and *prayer transitory*, as if *prier pour prier*, were all the Church of Rome did hold; and that they made no prayers to the saints, but only to pray for them The Bishop well remembers, that Master Casaubon more than once told him that reasoning with the Cardinal, touching the invocation of saints, the Cardinal freely confessed to him *that he had never prayed to saint in all his life, save only when he happened to follow the procession*, and that then he sung *Ora pro nobis* with the clerks indeed, *but else not*

"Which cometh much to this opinion he now seemeth to defend but wherein *others* of the Church of Rome will surely give him over, so that it is to be feared that the Cardinal will be shent for this, and *some censure come out against him* by the Sorbonne For the world cannot believe that *oblique relative* prayer is all that is sought, seeing it is most evident, by their breviaries, hours, and rosaries, that they pray *directly, absolutely, and finally to saints*, and make no mention at all of *prier pour prier*, to pray to God to forgive them; but to the saints, to give it themselves So that all he saith comes to nothing They say to the blessed Virgin, 'Sancta Maria,' not only 'Ora pro nobis,' but 'Succurre miseris, juva pusillanimes, resolve flebiles, accipe quod offerimus, dona quod rogamus, excusa quod timemus,' &c, &c   .   .   .   .

"All which, and many more, show plainly that the *practice* of the Church of Rome, in this point of invocation of saints is far otherwise than Cardinal Perron would bear the world in hand; and that *prier pour prier*, is not all, but that 'Tu dona cœlum, Tu laxa, Tu sana, Tu solve crimina, Tu duc, conduc, induc, perduc ad gloriam, Tu serva, Tu opem, Tu aufer, Tu confer vitam,' are said to them (*totidem verbis*)   *more than which cannot be said to* GOD *Himself.* And again, 'Hic nos solvat a peccatis, Hic nostros tergat reatus, Hic arma conferat, Hic hostem fuget, Hæc gubernet, Hic aptet tuo conspectui,' which if they be not *direct* and *absolute*, it would be asked of them, what is *absolute* or *direct ?*"— *Bishop Andrews's Answer to Chapter XX. of Cardinal Perron's Reply*, p 57–62.

Bellarmine's admissions quite bear out the principles laid down by Bishop Andrews and the Homilist :—

"It is not lawful," he says, "to ask of the saints to grant to us, as if they were the *authors* of divine benefits, glory or grace, or the other means of blessedness   . .   This is proved, first, from Scripture, 'The LORD will give grace and glory' (Psalm lxxxiv) Secondly, from the usage of the Church, for in the mass-prayers, and the saints' offices, we never ask any thing else, but at their prayers, benefits may be granted to us by GOD Thirdly, from reason , for *what we need surpasses the powers of the creature*, and therefore even of saints; therefore we ought to ask nothing of saints beyond their impetrating from GOD what is profitable for us   Fourthly, from Augustine and Theodoret, who expressly teach that saints are not to be invoked *as gods*, but as able to gain from GOD what they wish   However, it must be observed, when we say, that nothing should be asked of saints but their prayers for us, the question is not about the words, but the *sense* of the words   For, as far as words go, *it is lawful* to say   'St Peter, pity me, save me, open for me the gate of heaven,' also, 'give me health of body, patience, fortitude,' &c , provided that we mean 'save and pity me *by praying for me ,*' 'grant me this or that *by thy prayers and merits* '   For so speaks Gregory Nazianzen, and many others of the ancients," &c —*De Sanct Beat* , 1 17

[By the doctrine of the invocation of saints

then, the Article means all maintenance of addresses to them which intrench upon the incommunicable honors due to God alone, such as have been, and are in the Church of Rome, and such as, equally with the peculiar doctrine of purgatory, pardons, and worshipping and adoration of images and relics, as actually taught in that church, are unknown to the Catholic Church.]

By consulting Browne on the Articles, a work published since the above was written, very clear explanations of the Articles will be found.

§ 7.—*The Sacraments.*

ARTICLE XXV.—"Those five, commonly called Sacraments, that is to say, Confirmation, Penance, Orders, Matrimony, and Extreme Unction, are not to be counted for Sacraments of the Gospel, being such as have grown, partly of the corrupt following (pravâ imitatione) of the Apostles, partly from states of life allowed in the Scriptures; but yet have not like nature of sacraments (sacramentorum eandem rationem) with Baptism and the LORD's Supper, for that they have not any visible sign or ceremony ordained of God."

This Article does not deny the five rites in question to be sacraments, but to be sacraments in the *sense* in which Baptism and the LORD's Supper are sacraments; "sacraments of *the Gospel*," sacraments *with an outward sign ordained of God.*

They are not sacraments in *any* sense, *unless* the Church has the power of dispensing grace through rites of its own appointment, or is endued with the gift of blessing and hallowing the "rites or ceremonies" which, according to the twentieth

Article, it "hath power to decree." But we may well believe that the Church has this gift.

If, then, a sacrament be merely *an outward sign of an invisible grace given under it*, the five rites may be sacraments; but if it must be an outward sign *ordained by* GOD *or* CHRIST, then only Baptism and the LORD's Supper are sacraments.

Our Church acknowledges both definitions;— in the Article before us, *the stricter;* and again in the Catechism where a sacrament is defined to be " an outward visible sign of an inward spiritual grace, given unto us, *ordained by* CHRIST *Himself.*" And this, it should be remarked, is a characteristic of our formularies in various places, not to deny the *truth* or *obligation* of certain doctrines or ordinances, but simply to deny (what no Roman opponent now can successfully maintain), that CHRIST for certain directly ordained them. For instance, in regard to the visible Church it is sufficient that the ministration of the sacraments should be " *according to* CHRIST's *ordinance.*"— Art. xix. And it is added, " in all those things that *of necessity* are requisite to the same." The question entertained is, what is *the least* that GOD requires of us. Again, " the baptism of young children is to be retained, as most agreeable to *the institution of* CHRIST."—Art. xxvii. Again, " the sacrament of the Lord's Supper was not by CHRIST's *ordinance* reserved, carried about, lifted

up, or worshipped."—Art. xxviii.   Who will
maintain the paradox that what the Apostles " set
in order when they came" had been already done
by CHRIST?   Again, "both parts of the LORD's
sacrament, *by* CHRIST's *ordinance and commandment*, ought to be administered to all Christian
men alike."—Art. xxx.   Again, "bishops, priests,
and deacons, *are not commanded by* GOD's *law*
either to vow the estate of single life or to abstain
from marriage."—Art. xxxii.   [In making this
distinction, however, it is not here insinuated,
though the question is not entered on in these
particular Articles, that every one of these points,
of which it is only said that they are not ordained
by CHRIST, is justifiable on grounds short of His
appointment.]

On the other hand, our Church takes the *wider*
sense of the meaning of the word sacrament in the
Homilies ; observing—

" In the second Book against the Adversary of the Law and the
Prophets, he [St. Augustine] calleth sacraments *holy signs*   And
writing to Bonifacius of the baptism of infants, he saith, ' If sacraments had not a certain similitude of those things whereof they
be sacraments, they should be no sacrament at all   And of
this similitude they do for the most parts receive the names of
the self-same things they signify '   By these words of St Augustine it appeareth, that he alloweth the common description of a
sacrament, which is, that it is *a visible sign of an invisible grace;*
that is to say, that setteth out to the eyes and other outward
senses the inward working of GOD's free mercy, and doth, as it

4

were, seal in our hearts the promises of GOD."—*Homily on Common Prayer and Sacraments*, pp 296, 297.

Accordingly, starting with this definition of St. Augustine's, the writer is necessarily carried on as follows :—

"You shall hear how many sacraments there be, that were instituted by our SAVIOUR CHRIST, and are to be continued, and received of every Christian in due time and order, and for such purpose as our SAVIOUR CHRIST willed them to be received   And as for the number of them, if they should be considered according to the *exact* signification of a sacrament, namely, for visible signs expressly commanded in the New Testament, whereunto is annexed the promise of free forgiveness of our sins, and of our holiness and joining in CHRIST, there be but two, namely, Baptism, and the Supper of the LORD.   For although absolution hath the promise of forgiveness of sin, yet by the *express* word of the New Testament, it hath not this promise annexed and tied to the visible sign, which is imposition of hands   For this visible sign (I mean laying on of hands) is not *expressly* commanded in the New Testament to be used in absolution, as the visible signs in Baptism and the LORD'S Supper are   and therefore, absolution is no *such* sacrament as Baptism and the Communion are   And though the ordering of ministers hath this visible sign and promise, yet it lacks the promise of remission of sin, as all other sacraments besides the two above named do   Therefore neither it, nor any *other* sacrament else, be *such* sacraments as Baptism and the Communion are   But in a general acceptation, the name of a sacrament may be attributed to any thing, whereby an holy thing is signified   In which understanding of the word, the ancient writers have given this name, not only to the other five, commonly of late years taken and used for supplying the number of the seven sacraments, but also to divers and sundry other ceremonies, as to oil, washing of feet, and such like, not meaning thereby to repute them as sacraments, *in the same significa-*

tion that the two forenamed sacraments are. And therefore St. Augustine, weighing the true signification and exact meaning of the word, writing to Januarius, and also in the Third Book of Christian Doctrine, affirmeth, that the sacraments of the Christians, as they are most excellent in signification, so are they most few in number, and in both places maketh mention expressly of two, the sacrament of Baptism, and the Supper of the LORD. And although there are retained by order of the Church of England, besides these two, certain other rites and ceremonies, about the institution of ministers in the Church, Matrimony, Confirmation of Children, by examining them of their knowledge in the Articles of the Faith, and joining thereto the prayers of the Church for them, and likewise for the Visitation of the Sick yet no man ought to take these for sacraments, in *such* signification and meaning as the sacraments of Baptism and the LORD'S Supper are but either for godly states of life, necessary in CHRIST'S Church, and therefore worthy to be set forth by public action and solemnity, by the ministry of the Church, or else judged to be such ordinances as may make for the instruction, comfort, and edification of CHRIST'S Church "—*Homily on Common Prayer and Sacraments*, pp 298–300

Another definition of the word sacrament, which equally succeeds in limiting it to the two principal rites of the Christian Church, is also contained in the Catechism, as well as alluded to in the above passage:—" Two only, as *generally necessary* to salvation, Baptism and the Supper of the LORD." On this subject the following remark has been made:—

" The Roman Catholic considers that there are seven [sacraments]; we do not strictly determine the number. We define the word generally to be an ' outward sign of an inward grace,' without saying to how many ordinances this applies. However, what we do determine is, that CHRIST has ordained two special sacraments, as *generally necessary to salvation*. This, then, is the characteristic mark of those two, separating them from all other whatever; and this is nothing else but saying in other words that they are the only *justifying* rites, or instruments of communicating the Atonement, which is the one thing necessary to us. Ordination, for instance, gives *power*, yet without making the soul *acceptable* to GOD; Confirmation gives *light and strength*, yet is the mere *completion* of Baptism; and Absolution may be viewed as a negative ordinance removing the *barrier* which sin has raised between us and that grace, which by inheritance is ours. But the two sacraments 'of the Gospel,' as they may be emphatically styled, are the instruments of inward *life*, according to our LORD's declaration, that Baptism is a new *birth*, and that in the Eucharist we eat the *living* bread."

§ 8.—*Transubstantiation.*

ARTICLE XXVIII.—" Transubstantiation, or the change of the substance of bread and wine, in the Supper of the Lord, cannot be proved by Holy Writ ; but is repugnant to the plain words of Scripture, overthroweth the nature of a sacrament, and hath given occasion to many superstitions."

What is here opposed as " Transubstantiation," is the shocking doctrine that " the body of CHRIST," as the Article goes on to express it, is *not* " given, taken, and eaten, after an heavenly and spiritual manner, but is carnally pressed with the teeth ;" that it is a body or substance of a certain extension and bulk in space, and a certain figure and due disposition of parts, whereas we hold that the only substance such, is the bread which we see.

This is plain from Article xxix., which quotes St. Augustine as speaking of the wicked as " carnally and visibly pressing with their teeth the *sacrament* of the body and blood of CHRIST," not the real substance, a statement which even the

Breviary introduces into the service for Corpus Christi Day.

This is plain also from the words of the Homily: —" Saith Cyprian, ' When we do these things, *we need not whet our teeth*, but with sincere faith we break and divide that holy bread. It is well known that the meat we seek in this supper is spiritual food, the nourishment of the soul, a heavenly refection, *and not earthly ;* an invisible meat, *and not a bodily :* a ghostly substance, *and not carnal.'* "

Some extracts may be quoted to the same effect from Bishop Taylor. Speaking of what has been believed in the Church of Rome, he says :—

' Sometimes CHRIST hath appeared in His own shape, and blood and flesh hath been pulled out of the mouths of the communicants. and Plegilus, the priest, saw an angel, showing CHRIST to him in form of a child upon the altar, whom first he took in his arms and kissed, but did eat him up presently in his other shape, in the shape of a wafer ' Speciosa certè pax nebulonis, ut qui oris præbuerat basium, dentium inferret exitium,' said Berengarius ' It was but a Judas's kiss to kiss with the lip, and bite with the teeth ' "—*Bp Taylor*, vol. x. p 12

Again :—

" Yet if this and the other miracles pretended, had not been illusions or directly fabulous, it had made very much against the present doctrine of the Roman Church , for they represent the body in such measure, as by their explications it is not, and it cannot be , they represent it broken, a finger, or a piece of flesh, or bloody, or bleeding, or in the form of an infant   and then, when it is in the species of bread for if, as they say, CHRIST'S body is present no longer than the form of bread remained, how can it be CHRIST'S body in the miracle, when the species being gone, it is no longer a sacrament ?   But the dull inventors of miracles in those ages considered nothing of this , the article itself was then gross and rude, and so were the instruments of probation   I noted this, not only to show at what door so incredible a persuasion entered, but that the zeal of prevailing in it hath so blinded the refiners of it in this age, that they still urge these miracles for proof, when, if they do any thing at all, they reprove the present doctrine "—*Bp. Taylor's Works*, vol ix p ccccxi

Again : the change which is denied in the Article is accurately specified in another passage of the same author :—

" I will not insist upon the unworthy questions which this carnal doctrine introduces .   neither will I make scrutiny concerning CHRIST s bones, hair, and nails , nor suppose the Roman priests to be such καρχαρυδοντες, and to have such ' saws in their mouths,' these are appendages of their persuasion, but to be abominated by all Christian and modest persons, who use to eat not the bodies but the flesh of beasts, and not to devour, but to worship the body of CHRIST in the exaltation, and now in union with His divinity "—*On the Real Presence*, 11

And again :—

" They that *deny the spiritual sense*, and affirm the natural, are to remember that CHRIST reproved all senses of these words that were not *spiritual*   And by the way, let me observe, that the expressions of some chief men among the Romanists are so rude and crass, *that it will be impossible to excuse them from the understanding the words in the sense of the men of Capernaum ,* for, as they understood CHRIST to mean His ' true flesh natural and proper,' so do they   as they thought CHRIST intended they should *tear Him with their teeth and suck His blood,* for which they were offended , so do these men not only think so, but say so, and are not offended   So said Alanus, ' Assertissime loquimur, corpus Christi vere a nobis contrectari, manducari, circumgestari, *dentibus teri [ground by the teeth]*, *sensibiliter sacrificari [sensibly sacrificed*], non minus quam ante consecrationem panis' [not less than the bread before consecration] . . I thought that the Romanists had been glad to separate their own opinion from the carnal conceit of the men of Capernaum and the offended disciples . . . but I find that Bellarmine owns it, even in them, in their rude circumstances, for he affirms that 'CHRIST corrected them *not for supposing so*, but reproved them *for not believing it to be so* And indeed himself says as much " The body of CHRIST is *truly and properly manducated or chewed* with the body in the Eucharist,' and to take off the foulness of the expression, by avoiding a worse, he is pleased to speak nonsense · 'A thing may be manducated or chewed, though it be not attrite or broken' . . But Bellarmine adds, that if you will not allow him to say so, then he grants it in plain terms, that CHRIST'S body is chewed, *is attrite, or broken with the teeth*, and that not tropically, *but properly* . . How? under the species of bread, and invisibly "—*Ibid* , 3

Take again the statement of Ussher :—

"Paschasius Radbertus, who was one of the first setters forward of this doctrine in the West, spendeth a large chapter upon this point, wherein he telleth us, that CHRIST in the sacrament did show himself 'oftentimes in a visible shape, either in the form of a lamb, or in the color of flesh and blood; so that while the host was a breaking or an offering, a lamb in the priest's hands, and blood in the chalice should be seen as it were flowing from the sacrifice, that what lay hid in a mystery might to them that yet doubted be made manifest in a miracle ' . The first [tale] was . of a Roman matron, who found a piece of the sacramental bread turned into the fashion of a finger, all bloody; which afterwards, upon the prayers of St Gregory, was converted to its former shape again. The other two were first coined by the Grecian liars . The former of these is not only related there, but also in the legend of Simeon Metaphrastes (which is such another author among the Grecians as Jacobus de Voragine was among the Latins), in the life of Arsenius, . how that a little child was seen upon the altar, and an angel cutting him into small pieces with a knife, and receiving his blood into the chalice, as long as the priest was breaking the bread into little parts   The latter is of a certain Jew, receiving the sacrament at St Basil's hands, converted visibly into true flesh and blood "—*Ussher's Answer to a Jesuit*, pp 62–64.

Or the following :—

" When St Odo was celebrating the mass in the presence of certain of the clergy of Canterbury (who maintained that the bread and wine, after consecration, do remain in their former substance, and are not CHRIST'S true body and blood, but of a figure of it), when he was come to confraction, presently the fragments of the body of CHRIST, which he held in his hands, began to pour forth blood into the chalice   Whereupon he shed tears of joy, and beckoning to them that wavered in their faith, to come near and see the wonderful work of GOD, as soon as they beheld it they cried out, 'O holy Prelate! to whom the SON of GOD has been pleased to reveal Himself visibly in the flesh, pray for us, that the blood we see here present to our eyes, may again be changed, lest for our unbelief the Divine vengeance fall upon us '   He prayed accordingly, after which, looking in the chalice, he saw the species of bread and wine, where he had left blood   .

"St Wittekundus, in the administration of the Eucharist, saw a child enter into every one's mouth, playing and smiling when some received him, and with an abhorring countenance when he went into the mouths of others ; CHRIST thus showing this saint in His countenance, who were worthy, and who unworthy receivers."—*Johnson's Miracles of Saints*, pp. 27, 28.

The same doctrine was imposed by Nicholas the Second on Berengarius, as the confession of the latter shows, which runs thus :—

"I, Berengarius,   . anathematiz eevery heresy, and more particularly that of which I have hitherto been accused . . . I agree with the Roman Church .   that the bread and wine which are

4*

placed on the altar are, after consecration, not only a sacrament, but even the true body and blood of our LORD JESUS CHRIST, and that these are *sensibly*, and not merely sacramentally, but in truth, *handled and broken* by the hands of the priest, and *ground by the teeth* of the faithful."—*Bowden's Life of Gregory VII.*, vol. u. p 243

Another illustration of the sort of doctrine offered in the Article, may be given from Bellarmine, whose controversial statements have already been introduced in the course of the above ex: tracts. He thus opposes the doctrine of *introsusception*, which the spiritual view of the Real Presence naturally suggests :—

He observes, that there are "two particular opinions, false and erroneous, excogitated in the schools : that of Durandus, who thought it probable that the substance of the body of CHRIST in the Eucharist was *without magnitude ;* and that of certain ancients, which Occam seems afterwards to have followed, that though it has magnitude (which they think not really separable from substance), yet every part is so penetrated by every other, that the body of CHRIST is *without figure*, without distinction and order of parts." With this he contrasts the doctrine which, he maintains, is that of the Church of Rome as well as the general doctrine of the schools, that " in the Eucharist whole CHRIST exists *with magnitude* and *all accidents*, except that relation to a heavenly location which He has as He is in heaven, and

those things which are concomitants on His exist-
ence in that location; and that the parts and
members of CHRIST's body do *not* penetrate each
other, but are so distinct and arranged one with
another, as to have a *figure and order* suitable to
a human body.—*De Euchar.*, iii. 5.

We see then, that, by transubstantiation, our
Article does not confine itself to any abstract
theory, nor aim at any definition of the word substance, nor in rejecting it, rejects a word, nor in
denying a "mutatio panis et vini," is denying
every kind of change, but opposes itself to a certain plain and unambiguous statement, not of this
or that council, but one generally received or
taught both in the schools and in the multitude,
that the material elements are changed into an
earthly, fleshly, and organized body, extended in
size, distinct in its parts, which is there where the
outward appearances of bread and wine are, and
only does not meet the senses, nor even that
always.

Objections against "substance," "nature,"
"change," "accidents," and the like, seem more
or less questions of words, and inadequate expressions of the great offence which we find in the
received Roman view of this sacred doctrine.

In this connection it may be suitable to proceed

to notice the Explanation appended to the Communion Service, of our kneeling at the LORD's Supper, which requires explanation itself, more perhaps than any part of our formularies. It runs as follows :—

"Whereas it is ordained in this office for the Administration of the LORD's Supper, that the communicants should receive the same kneeling (which order is well meant, for a signification of our humble and grateful acknowledgment of the benefits of CHRIST therein given to all worthy receivers, and for the avoiding of such profanation and disorder in the Holy Communion, as might otherwise ensue); yet, lest the same kneeling should by any persons, either out of ignorance and infirmity, or out of malice and obstinacy, be misconstrued and depraved,—it is hereby declared, that thereby no adoration is intended, or ought to be done, either unto the sacramental bread or wine there bodily received, or unto any corporal presence of CHRIST's natural flesh and blood. For the sacramental bread and wine remain still in their very natural substances, and therefore may not be adored (for that were idolatry, to be abhorred of all faithful Christians); and the natural body and blood of our SAVIOUR CHRIST are in heaven, and not here, it being against the truth of CHRIST's natural body to be at one time in more places than one."

Now it may be admitted without difficulty, — 1. That "no adoration ought to be done unto the sacramental bread and wine there bodily received." 2. Nor "unto any *corporal* [*i. e.*, carnal] presence of CHRIST's natural flesh and blood." 3. That "the sacramental bread and wine remain still in their very natural substances." 4. That to adore them "were idolatry, to be abhorred of all faithful Christians;" and 5. That "the natural body and blood of our SAVIOUR CHRIST are in heaven."

But to "heaven" is added, "*and not here.*" Now, though it be allowed that there is no "*corporal* presence" [*i. e.*, carnal] of "CHRIST's natural flesh and blood" here, it is a further point to allow that "CHRIST's natural body and blood" are "*not here.*" And the question is, how can there be any *presence* at all of His body and blood, yet a presence such, as not to be *here?* How can there be any *presence*, yet not *local?*

Yet that this is the meaning of the paragraph in question is plain, from what it goes on to say in proof of its position: "It being against the truth of CHRIST's natural body to be at one time in more places than one." It is here asserted, then, 1. Generally, "no nature body can be in more places than one;" therefore, 2. CHRIST's natural body cannot be in the bread and wine, or there where the bread and wine are seen. In other words, there is no local presence in the Sa_ crament. Yet, that there is *a* presence, is asserted in the Homilies, as quoted above, and the question is, as just now stated, "How can there be a presence, yet not a local one?"

Now, first, let it be observed that the question to be solved is the truth of a certain philosophical deduction, not of a certain doctrine of Scripture. That there is a real presence, Scripture asserts, and the Homilies, Catechism, and Communion Service confess; but the Explanation before us adds, that it is philosophically impossible that it should be a particular kind of presence, a presence of which one can say, "It is here," or which is "local." It states then a philosophical deduction; but to such deduction none of us have subscribed. We have professed in the words of the Canon: "That the Book of Prayer, &c., containeth in it *nothing contrary to the word of* GOD." Now, a position like this may not be, and is not, "contrary to the word of GOD," and yet need not be true; *c. g.*, we may accept St. Clement's Epistle to the Corinthians, as containing nothing contrary to Scripture, nay, as altogether most scriptural, and yet this would not hinder us from rejecting the account of the Phœnix,—as contrary, not to GOD's word, but to matter of fact. Even the infallibility of the Roman see is not considered to extend to matters of fact or points of philosophy.

Nay, we commonly do not consider that we need take the words of Scripture itself literally about the sun's standing still, or the earth being fixed, or the firmament being above. Those at least who distinguish between what is theological in Scripture and what is scientific, and yet admit that Scripture is true, have no ground for wondering at such persons as subscribe to a paragraph, of which at the same time they disallow the philosophy; especially considering they expressly subscribe it only as not "contrary to the word of GOD." This then is what must be said first of all.

Next, the philosophical position is itself capable of a very specious defence. The truth is, we do not at all know what is meant by distance or intervals absolutely, any more than we know what is meant by absolute time. Late discoveries in geology have tended to make it probable that time may under circumstances go indefinitely faster or slower than it does at present; or, in other words, that indefinitely more may be accomplished in a given portion of it. What Moses calls a day, geologists wish to prove to be thousands of years, if we measure time by the operations at present effected in it. It is equally difficult to determine what we mean by distance, or why we should not be at this moment close to the throne of GOD, though we seem far from it. Our measure of distance is our hand or our foot; but as an object a foot off is not called

distant, though the interval is indefinitely divisible;
neither need it be distant either, after it has been
multiplied indefinitely. Why should any conven-
tional measure of ours—why should the perception
of our eyes or our ears, be the standard of presence
or distance? CHRIST may really be close to us,
though in heaven, and His presence in the Sacrament may but be a manifestation to the worshipper
of that nearness, not a change of place, which may
be unnecessary. But on this subject some extracts
may be suitably made from a pamphlet published
several years since, and admitting of one or two
verbal corrections, which, as in the case of other
similar quotations above, shall here be made without scruple :—

"In the note at the end of the Communion
Service, it is argued, that a body cannot be in two
places at once; and that therefore the Body of
CHRIST is not *locally* present, in the sense in which
we speak of the bread as being locally present.
On the other hand, in the Communion Service
itself, Catechism, Articles, and Homilies, it is
plainly declared, that the Body of CHRIST is in a
mysterious way, if not *locally*, yet *really* present,
so that we are able after some ineffable manner to
receive It. Whereas, then, the objection stands,
' CHRIST is not really here, because he is not locally
here,' our formularies answer, ' He is really here,
yet not locally.'

"But it may be asked, what is the meaning of saying that CHRIST is really present, yet not locally? I will make a suggestion on the subject. What do we mean by being *present?* How do we define and measure it? To a blind and deaf man, that only is present which he touches : give him hearing, and the range of things present enlarges ; every thing is present to him which he hears. Give him at length sight, and the sun may be said to be present to him in the daytime, and myriads of stars by night. The *presence*, then, of a thing is a relative word, depending, in a popular sense of it, upon the channel of communication between it and him to whom it is present ; and thus it is a word of degree.

"Such is the meaning of *presence*, when used of material objects ;—very different from this is the conception we form of the presence of spirit with spirit. The most intimate presence we can fancy is a spiritual presence in the soul ; it is nearer to us than any material object can possibly be ; for our body, which is the organ of conveying to us the presence of matter, sets bounds to its approach towards us. If, then, spiritual beings can be brought near to us (and that they can, we know, from what is told us of the influences of Divine grace, and again of evil angels upon our souls), their presence is something *sui generis*, of a more perfect and simple character than any presence we

commonly call local. And further, their presence
has nothing to do with the degrees of nearness:
they are either present or not present, or, in other
words, their coming is not measured by space, nor
their absence ascertained by distance. In the case
of things material, a transit through space is the
necessary condition of approach and presence; but
in things spiritual (whatever be the condition),
such a transit seems not to be a condition. The
condition is unknown. Once more: while beings
simply spiritual seem not to exist in place, the
Incarnate Son does; according to our Church's
statement already alluded to, that 'the natural
body and blood of our Saviour Christ are in
heaven, and not here, it being against the *truth*
of Christ's natural body to be at one time *in
more places than one.*'

"Such seems to be the mystery attending our
Lord and Saviour; He was a *body*, and that
spiritual. He is in place; and yet, as being a
Spirit, His mode of approach—the mode in which
He makes Himself present here or there—may
be, for what we know, as different from the mode
in which material bodies approach and come, as a
spiritual presence is more perfect. As material
bodies approach by moving from place to place,
so the approach and presence of a spiritual body
may be in some other way,—probably is in some
other way, since in some other way (as it would

appear), not gradual, progressive, approximating, that is, locomotive, but at once, spirits become present,—may be such as to be consistent with His remaining on GOD's right hand while He becomes present here,—that is, it may be real yet not local, or, in a word, is *mysterious*. The Body and Blood of CHRIST may be really, literally present in the Holy Eucharist, yet not having become present by local passage, may still literally and really be on GOD's right hand; so that, though they be present in deed and truth, it may be impossible, it may be untrue to say, that they are literally *in* the elements, or *about* them, or *in* the soul of the receiver. These may be useful modes of speech according to the occasion; but the true determination of all such questions may be this, that CHRIST's Body and Blood are *locally* at GOD's right hand, *yet* really *present* here,— present here, but not here in place,—because they are spirit.

" To assist our conceptions on this subject, I would recur to what I said just now about the presence of material objects, by way of putting my meaning in a different point of view. The presence of a material object, in the popular sense of the word, is a matter of degree, and ascertained by the means of apprehending it which belong to him to whom it is present. It is in some sense a correlative of the senses. A fly may be as near an edifice as a man; yet we do not call it present to the fly, because it cannot see it; and we call it present to the man because he can. This, however, is but a popular view of the matter: when we consider it carefully, it certainly is difficult to say what *is* meant by the presence of a material object relatively to us. It is in some respects truer to say that a thing is present, which is so circumstanced as to act upon us and influence us whether we are sensible of it or not. Now this is what the Catholic Church seems to hold concerning our LORD's Presence in the Sacrament, that He then personally and bodily is with us in the way an object is which we call present: how He is so, we know not, but that He should be so, though He be millions of miles away, is not more inconceivable than the influence of eyesight upon us is to a blind man. The stars are millions of miles off, yet they impress ideas upon our souls through our sight. We know of but five senses: we know not whether or not human nature be capable of more; we know not whether or not the soul possesses any thing analogous to them. We know nothing to negative the notion that the soul may be capable of having CHRIST present to it by the stimulating of dormant, or the development of possible energies.

" As sight for certain purposes annihilates space, so other unknown capacities, bodily or spiritual, may annihilate it for other purposes. Such a

practical annihilation was involved in the appearance of CHRIST to St. Paul on his conversion.
Such a practical annihilation was involved in the
doctrine of CHRIST'S ascension; to speak according
to the ideas of space and time commonly received,
what must have been the rapidity of that motion
by which, within ten days, He placed our human
nature at the right hand of GOD? Is it more
mysterious that He should 'open the heavens,' to
use the Scripture phrase, in the Sacramental rite;
that He should then dispense with time and space,
in the sense in which they are daily dispensed
with, in the sun's warming us at the distance of
100,000,000 of miles, than that He should have
dispensed with them on occasion of His ascending
on high? He who showed what the passage of an
incorruptible body was ere it had reached GOD's
throne, thereby suggests to us what may be its
coming back and presence with us now, when at
length glorified and become spirit.

"In answer, then, to the problem, *how* CHRIST
comes to u: while remaining on high, I answer
just as much as this,—that He comes by the
agency of the HOLY GHOST, *in* and *by the Sacrament*. Locomotion is the means of a material
Presence; the Sacrament is the means of His
spiritual Presence. As faith is the means of our
receiving It, so the HOLY GHOST is the Agent and
the Sacrament the means of His imparting It;

and therefore we call It a Sacramental Presence.
We kneel before His heavenly Throne, and the
distance is as nothing; it is as if that Throne were
the Altar close to us.

"Let it be carefully observed, that I am not
proving or determining any thing; I am only
showing how it is that certain propositions which
at first sight seem contradictions in terms, are not
so,—I am but pointing out *one* way of reconci-
ling them. If there is but one way assignable, the
force of all antecedent objection against the possibility of any at all is removed, and then of course
there may be other ways supposable though not
assignable. It seems at first sight a mere idle
use of words to say that CHRIST is really and literally, yet not locally, present in the Sacrament;
that He is there given to us, not in figure but in
truth, and yet is still only on the right hand of
GOD. I have wished to remove this seeming impossibility.

"If it be asked, *why* attempt to remove it, I
answer that I have no wish to do so, if persons
will not urge it against the Catholic doctrine.
Men maintain it as an impossibility, a contradiction in terms, and force a believer in it to say
why it should not be so accounted. And then
when he gives a reason, they turn round and
accuse him of subtleties, and refinements, and
scholastic trifling. Let them but believe and

act on the truth that the consecrated bread is
CHRIST's Body, as He says, and no officious comment on His words will be attempted by any
well-judging mind. But when they say 'this
cannot be literally true, *because* it is impossible;'
then they force those who think it is literally true,
to explain how, according to their notions, it is
not impossible. And those who ask hard questions must put up with hard answers."

There is nothing, then, in the Explanatory
Paragraph which has given rise to these remarks,
to interfere with the doctrine, elsewhere taught
in our formularies, of a real super-local presence
in the Holy Sacrament.

§ 9.—*Masses.*

Article XXXI.—"The sacrifice (sacrificia) of Masses, in which it was commonly said, that the priests did offer Christ for the quick and the dead, to have remission of pain or guilt, were blasphemous fables and dangerous deceits (perniciosæ imposturæ)."

Nothing can show more clearly than this passage, that the Articles are not written against the creed of the Roman Church, but against actual existing errors in it, whether taken into its system or not. Here the sacrifice of the *Mass* is not spoken of, in which the special question of doctrine would be introduced; but "the sacrifice of *Masses*," certain observances, for the most part private and solitary, which the writers of the Articles knew to have been in force in time past, and saw before their eyes, and which involved certain opinions and a certain teaching. Accordingly the passage proceeds, "in which it *was commonly said;*" which surely is a strictly historical mode of speaking.

If any testimony is necessary in aid of what is so plain from the wording of the Article itself, it is found in the drift of the following passage from Burnet:—

"It were easy from all the rituals of the ancients to show, that they had none of those ideas that are now in the Roman Church They had but one altar in a church, and probably but one in a city; they had but one communion in a day at that altar so far were they from the many altars in every church, and *the many masses* at every altar, that are now in the Roman Church They did not know what *solitary masses* were, without a communion. All the liturgies and all the writings of ancients are as express in this matter as is possible The whole constitution of their worship and discipline shows it Their worship always concluded with the Eucharist · such as were not capable of it, as the catechumens, and those who were doing public penance for their sins, assisted at the more general parts of the worship, and so much of it was called their mass, because they were dismissed at the conclusion of it When that was done, then the faithful stayed, and did partake of the Eucharist, and at the conclusion of it they were likewise dismissed, from whence it came to be called the mass of the faithful"

These sacrifices are said to be "blasphemous fables and pernicious impostures." Now the "blasphemous fable" is the teaching that there is a sacrifice for sin other than CHRIST's death, and that masses are that sacrifice. And the "pernicious imposture" is the turning this belief into a means of filthy lucre.

1. That the "blasphemous fable" is the teaching that masses are sacrifices for sin distinct from the sacrifice of CHRIST's death, is plain from the first sentence of the Article. "The offering of

5

CHRIST *once made*, is that perfect redemption, propitiation, and satisfaction for *all* the sins of the *whole world, both original and actual.* And *there is none other* satisfaction for sin, but *that alone. Wherefore* the sacrifice of masses, &c." It is observable too that the heading of the Article runs, "Of the one oblation of CHRIST finished upon the Cross," which interprets the *drift* of the statement contained in it about masses.

Our Communion Service shows it also, in which the prayer of consecration commences pointedly with a declaration, which has the force of a protest, that CHRIST made on the cross "by His *one* oblation of Himself *once* offered, a *full, perfect,* and *sufficient* sacrifice, oblation, and *satisfaction* for the sins of the whole world."

And again in the offering of the sacrifice: "We entirely desire thy fatherly goodness mercifully to accept our sacrifice of praise and thanksgiving, most humbly beseeching Thee to grant that *by the merits and death of Thy* SON JESUS CHRIST, and through faith in His blood, we and all Thy whole Church may obtain *remission of our sins* and all *other benefits* of His Passion."

[And in the notice of the celebration: "I purpose, through God's assistance, to administer to all such as shall be religiously and devoutly disposed, the most comfortable Sacrament of the Body and Blood of CHRIST; to be by them received in remembrance of His meritorious Cross and Passion; *whereby alone* we obtain remission of our sins, and are made partakers of the kingdom of heaven."]

But the popular charge still urged against the Roman system as introducing in the mass a second or rather continually recurring atonement, is a sufficient illustration, without further quotations, of this part of the Article.

2. That the "blasphemous and pernicious imposture" is the turning the Mass into a gain, is plain from such passages as the following :—

"With what earnestness, with what vehement zeal, did our SAVIOUR CHRIST drive the buyers and sellers out of the temple of GOD, and hurl down the tables of the changers of money, and the seats of the dove-sellers, and could not abide that a man should carry a vessel through the temple He told them, that they had made His FATHER'S house a den of thieves, partly through their superstition, hypocrisy, false worship, false doctrine, and insatiable covetousness, and partly through contempt, abusing that place with walking and talking, with worldly matters, without all fear of GOD, and due reverence to that place. What dens of thieves the churches of England have been made by the *blasphemous buying and selling the most precious body and blood of* CHRIST *in the Mass*, as the world was made to believe, at dirges, at months minds, at trentalls, in abbeys and chantries, besides other horrible abuses, (GOD'S holy name be blessed forever!) which we now see and understand All these abominations they that supply the room of CHRIST have cleansed and purged the churches of England of, taking away all such fulsomeness and filthiness, as through blind devotion and ignorance hath crept into the Church these many hundred years "—*On repairing and keeping clean of Churches*, pp 229, 230.

Other passages are as follows :—

"Have not the Christians of late days, and even in our days also, in like manner provoked the displeasure and indignation of ALMIGHTY GOD, partly because they have profaned and defiled their churches with heathenism and Jewish abuses, with images and idols, with numbers of altars, too superstitiously and intolerably abused, with gross abusing and filthy corrupting of the LORD'S Holy Supper, the blessed Sacrament of His body and blood, with an infinite number of toys and trifles of their own devices, to make a goodly outward show, and to deface the homely, simple, and sincere religion of CHRIST JESUS, partly, they resort to the church like hypocrites, full of all iniquity and sinful life, having a vain and dangerous fancy and persuasion, that if they come to the church, besprinkle them with holy water, *hear a mass, and be blessed with a chalice,* though they understand not one word of the whole service. nor feel one motion of repentance in the heart, all is well, all is sure?"—*On the Place and Time of Prayer,* p 293

Again :—

"What hath been the cause of this gross idolatry, but the ignorance hereof? What hath been the cause of this *mummish massing,* but the ignorance hereof? Yea, what hath been, and what is at this day the cause of this want of love and charity, but the ignorance hereof? Let us therefore so travail to understand the LORD'S Supper, that we be no cause of the decay of GOD'S worship, of no idolatry, of no *dumb massing,* of no hate and malice, so may we the boldlier have access thither to our comfort."—*Homily concerning the Sacrament,* pp. 377, 378

To the same purpose is the following passage from Bishop Bull's Sermons :—

"It were easy to show, how the whole frame of religion and doctrine of the Church of Rome, as it is distinguished from that Christianity which we hold in common with them, is evidently designed and contrived *to serve the interest and profit* of them that rule that Church, by the disservices, yea, and ruin of those souls that are under their government . . . What can the doctrine of men's playing an after-game for their salvation in purgatory be designed for, but to enhance *the price of the priest's masses* and dirges for the dead? Why must a *solitary* mass, *bought for a piece of money*, performed and participated by a priest alone, in a private corner of a church, be, not only against the sense of Scripture and the Primitive Church, but also against common sense and grammar, called a communion, and be accounted useful to him that buys it, though he never himself receive the sacrament, or but once a year, but for this reason, that there is *great gain* but no godliness at all, in this doctrine?"—*Bp. Bull's Sermons*, p 10

And Burnet says :—

"Without going far in tragical expressions, we cannot hold saying what our SAVIOUR said upon another occasion, 'My house is a house of prayer, but ye have made it a den of thieves' A trade was set up on this foundation The world was made believe, that by the virtue of so many *masses, which were to be purchased by great endowments*, souls were redeemed out of purgatory, and scenes of visions and apparitions, sometimes of the tormented, and sometimes of the delivered souls, were published in all places which had so wonderful an effect, that in the two or three centuries, *endowments* increased to so vast a degree, that if the scandals of the clergy on the one hand, and the statutes of mortmain on the other, had not restrained the profuseness that the world was wrought up to on this account, it is not easy to imagine how far this might have gone, perhaps to an entire subjecting of the temporality to the spirituality The practices by which this was managed, and the effects that followed on it, we can call by no other name than downright *impostures*, worse than the making or vending false coin, when the world was drawn in by such arts to plain bargains, to *redeem* their own souls, and the souls of their ancestors and posterity, *so many masses were to be said*, and forfeitures to follow upon their not being said. thus the *masses were really the price* of the lands."

The truth of these representations cannot be better shown than by extracting the following passage from the Session 22 of the Council of Trent:—

"Whereas, many things appear to have crept in heretofore, whether by the fault of the times or by the neglect and wickedness of men, foreign to the dignity of so great a sacrifice, in order that it may regain to due honor and observance, to the glory of GOD and the edification of His faithful people, the Holy Council decrees, that the bishops, ordinaries of each place, diligently take care and be bound to forbid and put an end to all those things, which either *avarice*, which is idolatry, or *irreverence*, which is scarcely separable from impiety, or *superstition*, the pretence of true piety, has introduced. And, to say much in a few words, first of all, as to avarice, let them altogether forbid agreements and bargains of *payment* of whatever kind, and *whatever is given for celebrating new masses*, moreover, importunate and mean extortion, rather than petition of alms, and such like practices, which border on simoniacal sin certainly on *filthy lucre.* . . . . And let them banish from the church those musical practices, *when with the organ or with the chant any thing lascivious or impure is mingled*, also all secular practices, vain and therefore profane conversations, promenadings, bustle, clamor, so that the house of GOD may truly seem and be called the house of prayer Lastly, lest any opening be given to superstition, let them provide by edict and punishments appointed, that the priests celebrate it at no other than the due hours, nor use rites or ceremonies and prayers in the celebration of masses, other than those which have been approved by the Church, and received on frequent and laudable use And let them altogether remove from the Church a *set number of certain masses and candles*, which has proceeded rather from *superstitious observance* than from true religion, and teach the people in what consists, and from whom, above all, proceeds the so precious and heavenly fruit of this most holy sacrifice And let them admonish the same people to come frequently to their parish churches, at least on Sundays and the greater feasts," &c

On the whole, then, it is conceived that the Article before us neither speaks against the Mass in itself, nor against its being [an offering, though commemorative]* for the quick and the dead for the remission of sin [(especially since the decree of Trent says, that "the fruits of the Bloody Oblation are through this most abundantly obtained; so far is the latter from detracting in any way from the former")]; but against its being viewed, on the one hand, as independent of or distinct from the sacrifice on the Cross, which is blasphemy, and on the other, its being directed to the emolument of those to whom it pertains to celebrate it, which is imposture in addition.

Fuller quotations might be taken from Browne on the Articles, but it is intended to reprint this just as the original, in which Bishop Browne's work could not be quoted, as it was not published

---

* " An offering for the quick," &c —*First Edition*

§ 10.—*Marriage of Clergy.*

ARTICLE XXXII.—" Bishops, Priests and Dea. cons, are not commanded by GOD's law, either to vow the estate of single life, or to abstain from marriage."

There is literally no subject for controversy in these words, since even the most determined advocates of the celibacy of the clergy admit their truth. [As far as clerical celibacy is a duty, it] is grounded not on GOD's law, but on the Church's rule, or on vow. No one, for instance, can question the vehement zeal of St. Jerome in behalf of this observance, yet he makes the following admission in his attack upon Jovinian :—

"Jovinian says, 'You speak in vain, since the Apostle appointed Bishops, and Presbyters, and Deacons, the husbands of one wife, and having children' But, as the Apostle says, that he has not a precept concerning virgins, yet gives a counsel as having received mercy of the LORD, and urges throughout that discourse a preference of virginity to marriage, and *advises what he does not command*, lest he seem to cast a snare, and to impose a burden too great for man's nature, *so also*, in ecclesiastical order, seeing that an infant Church was then forming out of the Gentiles, he gives the lighter precepts to recent converts, lest they should fall under them through fear."—*Adv Jovinian,* 1 34

And the Council of Trent merely lays down :—

" If any shall say that clerks in holy orders, or regulars, who have solemnly professed chastity, can contract matrimony, and that the contract is valid, *in spite of ecclesiastical law or vow*, let him be anathema "—*Sess* 24, *Can.* 9.

Here the observance is placed simply upon rule of the Church or upon vow, neither of which exists in the English Church; "*therefore*," as the Article logically proceeds, "it *is* lawful for them, as for all other Christian men, to marry *at their own discretion*, as they shall judge the same to serve better to godliness." Our Church leaves the discretion with the clergy; and most persons will allow that, *under our circumstances*, she acts wisely in doing so. That she has *power*, did she so choose, to take from them this discretion, and to oblige them either to marriage [(as is said to be the case as regards the parish priests of the Greek Church)] or to celibacy, would seem to be involved in the doctrine of the following extract from the Homilies; though, whether an enforcement either of the one or the other rule would be expedient and pious, is another matter. Speaking of fasting, the Homily says :—

"GOD'S Church ought not, neither may it be so tied to that or any other order now made, or hereafter to be made and devised by the authority of man, but *that it may lawfully, for just causes, alter, change, or mitigate* those ecclesiastical decrees and orders, yea, *recede wholly from them and break them*, when they tend either to superstition or to impiety, when they draw the people from GOD rather than work any edification in them This authority CHRIST Himself used and *left it to* His Church. He used it, I say, for the

5*

order or decree made by the elders for washing ofttimes, which was diligently observed of the Jews; yet tending to superstition, our SAVIOUR CHRIST altered and changed the same in His Church into a profitable sacrament, the sacrament of our regeneration or new birth. This authority to mitigate laws and decrees ecclesiastical, the Apostles practised, when they, writing from Jerusalem unto the congregation that was at Antioch, signified unto them that they would not lay any further burden upon them, but these necessaries that is, 'that they should abstain from things offered unto idols, from blood, from that which is strangled, and from fornication,' notwithstanding that Moses's law required many other observances. This authority to change the orders, decrees, and constitutions of the Church was after the Apostles' time, used of the Fathers about the manner of fasting, as it appeareth in the Tripartite History . Thus ye have heard, good people, first, that Christian subjects are bound even in conscience to obey princes' laws, which are not repugnant to the laws of GOD Ye have also heard that CHRIST's Church is not so bound to observe any order, law, or decree made by man, to prescribe a form in religion, but that the Church hath full power and authority from GOD to change and alter the same, when need shall require, which hath been showed you by the example of our SAVIOUR, CHRIST, by the practice of the Apostles, and of the Fathers since that time "—*Homily on Fasting,* 242–244

To the same effect the 34th Article declares that,

" It is not necessary that traditions and ceremonies be in all places one, and utterly like, for at all times they have been divers, and *may be changed* according to diversities of countries, times, and men's manners, so that nothing be ordained against GOD's Word Whosoever, *through his private judgment,* willingly and purposely doth openly *break* the traditions and ceremonies of the Church, which be not repugnant to the word of GOD, and be ordained and approved by common authority, ought to be rebuked openly "—*Article* XXXIV

§ 11.—*The Homilies.*

ARTICLE XXXV.—" The second Book of Homilies doth contain a godly and wholesome doctrine, and necessary for these times, as doth the former Book of Homilies."

This Article has been treated of in No. 82 of these Tracts, in the course of an answer given to an opponent, who accused its author of not fairly receiving the Homilies, because he dissented from their doctrine, that the Bishop of Rome is Antichrist, and that regeneration was vouchsafed under the law. The passage of the Tract shall here be inserted, with some abridgment.

" I say plainly, then, I have not *subscribed* the Homilies, nor was it ever intended that any member of the English Church should be subjected to what, if considered as an extended confession, would indeed be a yoke of bondage. Romanism surely is innocent, compared with that system which should impose upon the conscience a thick octavo volume, written flowingly and freely by fallible men, to be received exactly, sentence by sentence : I cannot conceive any grosser instance of a pharisaical tradition than this would be. No; such a proceeding would render it impossible (I will say) for any one member, lay or clerical, of the Church to remain in it, who was subject to such an ordeal. For instance: I do not suppose that any reader would be satisfied with the political reasons for fasting, though indirectly introduced, yet fully admitted and dwelt upon in the Homily on that subject. He would not like to subscribe the declaration that eating fish was a duty, not only as being a kind of fasting, but as making provisions cheap, and encouraging the fisheries. He would not like the association of religion with earthly politics.

"How, then, are we bound to the Homilies? By the Thirty-fifth Article, which speaks as follows: 'The second Book of Homilies . . . doth *contain* a godly and wholesome *doctrine*, and necessary for these times, as doth the former *Book of Homilies*.' Now, observe, this Article does not speak of every statement made in them, but of the '*doctrine*.' It speaks of the *view* or *cast*, or *body of doctrine* contained in them. In spite of ten thousand incidental propositions, as in any large book, there is, it is obvious, a certain line of doctrine, which may be contemplated continuously in its shape and direction. For instance: if you say you disapprove the doctrine contained in the Tracts for the Times, no one supposes you to mean that every sentence and half sentence is a lie. I say then, that, in like manner, when the Article speaks of the *doctrine* of the Homilies, it does not measure the letter of them by the inch, it does not imply that they contain no propositions which admit of two opinions; but it speaks of a certain determinate line of doctrine, and moreover adds, it is '*necessary for these times.*' Does not *this*, too, show the same thing? If a man said, the Tracts for the Times are *seasonable* at this moment, as their title signifies, would he not speak of them as taking a certain line, and bearing in a certain way? Would he not be speaking, not of phrases or sentences, but of a 'doctrine' in them tending one way, viewed as a whole? Would he be inconsistent, if, after praising them as seasonable, he continued, ' yet I do not pledge myself to every view or sentiment; there are some things in them hard of digestion, or overstated, or doubtful, or subtle ?'

" If any thing could add to the irrelevancy of the charge in question, it is the particular point in which it is urged that I dissent from the Homilies,— a question concerning the fulfilment of prophecy, viz., whether Papal Rome is Antichrist ! An iron yoke indeed you would forge for the conscience, when you oblige us to assent, not only to all matters of *doctrine* which the Homilies contain, but even to their opinion concerning the fulfilment of prophecy. Why, *wo* do not ascribe authority in such matters even to the unanimous consent of all the Fathers.

"I will put what I have been saying in a second point of view. The Homilies are subsidiary to the Articles; therefore they are of authority so far as they *bring out* the sense of the Articles, and are not of authority where they do not. For instance, they say that David, though unbaptized, was regenerated, as you have quoted. This statement cannot be of authority, because it not only does not agree, but it even disagrees, with the Ninth Article, which translates the Latin word 'renatis' by the English 'baptized.' But, observe, if this mode of viewing the Homilies be taken, as it fairly may, *you* suffer from it; for the Apocrypha, *being the subject of an Article*, the comment furnished in the Homily is binding on you, whereas you reject it.

"A further remark will bring us to the same point. Another test of acquiescence in the doctrine of the Homilies is this:—Take their table of contents; examine the headings; these surely, taken together, will give the substance of their teaching. Now I hold fully and heartily the doctrine of the Homilies, under every one of these headings: the only points to which I should not accede, nor think myself called upon to accede, would be certain matters, subordinate to the doc-

trines to which the headings refer—matters not
of doctrine, but of opinions, as, that Rome is the
Antichrist; or of historical fact, as, that there
was a Pope Joan. But now, on the other hand,
can *you* subscribe the doctrine of the Homilies
under every one of its formal headings? I believe
you *cannot*. The Homily against Disobedience
and Wilful Rebellion is, in many of its element-
ary principles, decidedly uncongenial with your
sentiments."

This illustration of the subject may be thought
enough; yet it may be allowable to add from the
Homilies a number of propositions and statements
of more or less importance, which are too much
forgotten at this day, and are decidedly opposed
to the views of certain schools of religion, which
at the present moment are so eager in claiming
the Homilies to themselves. This is not done, as
the extract already read will show, with the inten-
tion of maintaining that they are one and all
binding on the conscience of those who subscribe
the Thirty-fifth Article; but since the strong language of the Homilies against the Bishop of Rome
is often quoted, as if it were thus proved to be the
doctrine of our Church, it may be as well to show
that, following the same rule, we shall be also
introducing Catholic doctrines, which indeed it
far more belongs to a Church to profess than a
certain view of prophecy, but which do not ap-

prove themselves to those who hold it. For instance, we read as follows:—

1. "The great clerk and godly preacher, St. John Chrysostom."—1 B. i. 1. And, in like manner, mention is made elsewhere of St. Augustine, St. Ambrose, St. Hilary, St. Basil, St. Cyprian, St. Hierome, St. Martin, Origen, Prosper, Ecumenius, Photius, Bernardus, Anselm, Didymus, Theophylactus, Tertullian, Athanasius, Lactantius, Cyrillus, Epiphanius, Gregory, Irenæus, Clemens, Rabanus, Isidorus, Eusebius, Justinus Martyr, Optatus, Eusebius, Emissenus, and Bede.

2. "Infants, being baptized, and dying in their infancy, are by this Sacrifice washed from their sins . . . and they, which in act or deed do sin after this baptism, when they turn to God unfeignedly, they are *likewise* washed by this Sacrifice," &c.—1 B. iii. 1. *init.*

3. "Our office is, not to pass the time of this present life unfruitfully and idly, after that we are *baptized or justified*," &c.—1 B. iii. 3.

4. "By holy promises, we be made lively members of Christ, receiving the sacrament of Baptism. By like holy promises *the sacrament of Matrimony* knitteth man and wife in perpetual love."—1 B. vii. 1.

5. "Let us learn also here [in the Book of Wisdom] by *the infallible and undeceivable Word of* God, that," &c.—1 B. x, 1.

6. " The due receiving of His blessed Body and Blood, *under the form* of bread and wine."— *Note at end of* B. i.

7. "In the Primitive Church, *which was most holy and godly* . . . open offenders were not suffered once to enter into the house of the LORD . . . until they had done open penance . . . but this was practised, not only upon mean persons, but also upon the *rich, noble, and mighty persons,* yea, upon Theodosius, *that puissant and mighty Emperor,* whom . . . . St. Ambrose . . . . did . . . . excommunicate."—2 B. i. 2.

8. "Open offenders were not . . . admitted to common prayer, and the use of the holy *sacraments.*"—*Ibid*

9. "Let us amend this our negligence and contempt in coming to the house of the LORD ; and resorting thither diligently together, let us there . . . celebrating also reverently the LORD's holy *sacraments*, serve the LORD in His holy house."— *Ibid*. 5.

10. "Contrary to the . . . most manifest doctrine of the Scriptures, and contrary to the usage of the Primitive Church, *which was most pure and uncorrupt*, and contrary to the sentences and judgments of the *most ancient, learned, and godly* doctors of the Church."—2 B. ii. 1, *init.*

11. "This truth . . . was believed and taught by the *old holy Fathers*, and *most ancient learned*

doctors, and received by the old Primitive Church, *which was most uncorrupt and pure.*"—2 B. ii. 2, *init.*

12. "Athanasius, a very ancient, holy, and learned bishop and doctor."—*Ibid.*

13. "Cyrillus, an old and holy doctor."—*Ibid.*

14. "Epiphanius, Bishop of Salamine, in Cyprus, a very holy and learned man."—*Ibid.*

15. "To whose (Epiphanius's) judgment you have . . . all the learned and godly bishops and clerks, yea, and the whole Church of that age" [the Nicene], "and so upward to our SAVIOUR CHRIST's time, by the space of about four hundred years, consenting and agreeing."—*Ibid.*

16. "Epiphanius, a bishop and doctor of such antiquity, holiness, and authority."—*Ibid.*

17. "St. Augustine, the best learned of all ancient doctors."—*Ibid.*

18. "That ye may know why and when, and by whom images were first used privately, and afterwards not only received into Christian churches and temples, but, in conclusion, worshipped also ; and how the same was gainsaid, resisted, and forbidden, as well by *godly bishops and learned doctors*, as also by sundry Christian princes, I will briefly collect," &c. [The bishops and doctors which follow are:] "St. Jerome, Serenus, Gregory, the Fathers of the Council of Eliberis."

19. "Constantine, Bishop of Rome, assembled

a Council of bishops of the West, and did condemn Philippicus, *the Emperor*, and John, Bishop of Constantinople, of the *heresy of the Monothelites*, not without a cause indeed, but *very justly.*"—*Ibid.*

20. " Those six Councils, *which were allowed and received of all men.*"—*Ibid.*

21. " There were no images publicly by the space of almost *seven hundred years*. And there is *no doubt* but the Primitive Church, next the Apostles' times, was *most pure.*"—*Ibid.*

22. " Let us beseech GOD that we, being *warned* by His Holy Word . . . and by *the writings of old godly doctors* and ecclesiastical histories," &c.—*Ibid.*

23. " It shall be declared, both by GOD's Word, and the *sentences* of the ancient doctors, and *judgment* of the Primitive Church," &c.—2 B. ii. 3.

24. "Saints, whose souls *reign* in joy with GOD."—*Ibid.*

25. "That the law of GOD is likewise to be *understood* against all our images . . . appeareth further by the *judgment* of the old doctors and the Primitive Church."—*Ibid.*

26. " The Primitive Church, *which is specially to be followed*, as most incorrupt and pure."—*Ibid.*

27. " Thus it is declared by GOD's Word, the *sentences* of the doctors, and the *judgment* of the Primitive Church."—*Ibid.*

28. " The rude people, who specially, as the *Scripture* teacheth, are in danger of superstition and idolatry; viz., Wisdom xiii. xiv."—*Ibid*.

29. " They [the ' learned and holy bishops and doctors of the Church' of the first eight centuries] were the preaching bishops . . . And as they were most zealous and diligent, so were they of excellent learning and godliness of life, and by both of great authority and credit with the people."—*Ibid*.

30. " The most virtuous and best learned, the most diligent also, and in number almost infinite, ancient Fathers, bishops, and doctors . . . . could do nothing against images and idolatry."—*Ibid*.

31. " As the *Word of* God testifieth, Wisdom xiv."—*Ibid*.

32. " The saints *now reigning in heaven* with God."—*Ibid*.

33. " The *fountain of our generation* is there [in God's house] presented unto us."—2 B. iii.

36. " Somewhat shall now be spoken of one particular good work, whose commendation is both in the law and in the Gospel [fasting]."—2 B. iv. 1.

37. " If any man shall say . . . we are not now under the yoke of the law, we are set at liberty by the freedom of the Gospel; therefore these rites and customs of the old law bind not us, except it can be showed by the Scriptures of the New

Testament or by examples out of the same, that fasting, now under the Gospel, is a *restraint of meat, drink, and all bodily food and pleasures from the body*, as before : first, that we ought to fast, is a *truth more manifest, than it should here need to be proved* . . . Fasting, even by CHRIST's assent, is a withholding meat, drink, and all natural food from the body," &c.—*Ibid.*

38. " That it [fasting] was used in the Primitive Church, appeareth most evidently by the Chalcedon Council, one of the *four first general councils.* The Fathers assembled there . . . decreed in that council that every person, as well in his private as public fast, should continue all the day without meat and drink, till after the evening prayer. . . . This Canon teacheth how fasting was used in the Primitive Church."—*Ibid.* [The Council was A. D. 452.]

39. " Fasting then, by the *decree* of those 630 Fathers, *grounding* their determinations in this matter upon the sacred Scriptures . . . is a withholding of meat, drink, and all natural food from the body for the determined time of fasting."— *Ibid.*

40. " The order or decree made by the elders for washing ofttimes, tending to superstition, our SAVIOUR CHRIST altered and changed the same in His Church, into a profitable sacrament, the sacrament of our *regeneration or new birth*."—2 B. iv. 2.

41. "Fasting thus used with prayer is of *great efficacy* and *weigheth much* with God, so the angel Raphael told Tobias."—*Ibid.*

42. "As he" [St. Augustine] "witnesseth in another place, the martyrs and holy men in times past, were wont after their death to be *remembered* and *named* of the priest at divine service; but never to be invocated or called upon."—2 B. vii. 2.

43. "Thus you see that the *authority both* of Scripture and *also* of Augustine, doth not permit that we should pray to them."—*Ibid.*

44. "To temples have the *Christians* customably used to resort from time to time as to most meet places, where they might . . . receive His holy *sacraments* ministered unto them duly and purely."—2 B. viii. 1.

45. "The which thing both CHRIST and His Apostles, *with all the rest of the holy Fathers*, do sufficiently declare so."—*Ibid.*

46. "Our godly *predecessor*, and the *ancient* Fathers of the Primitive Church, spared not their goods to build churches."—*Ibid.*

47. "If we will show ourselves true Christians, if we will be followers of CHRIST our MASTER, and of those *godly Fathers* that have lived before us, and now have received the reward of true and faithful Christians," &c.—*Ibid.*

48. "We must . . . come unto the material

churches and temples to pray . . . . whereby we may reconcile ourselves to God, be partakers of His holy *sacraments*, and be devout hearers of His holy word," &c.—*Ibid.*

49. " It [ordination] lacks the promise of remission of sin, as all *other* sacraments besides the two above named do. Therefore, neither it, nor any *other* sacrament else, be *such* sacraments as Baptism and the Communion are."—2 *Hom.* ix.

50. " Thus we are taught both by the Scriptures and ancient doctors, that," &c.—*Ibid.*

51. " The holy Apostles and disciples of CHRIST . . . the godly Fathers also, that were both *before* and *since* CHRIST, *endued without doubt with the* HOLY GHOST, . . . they both do most earnestly exhort us, &c. . . . that we should remember the poor . . . St. Paul crieth unto us after this sort . . . Isaiah the Prophet teacheth us on this wise . . . . *And the holy Father Tobit* giveth this counsel . . . And *the learned and godly doctor Chrysostom*, giveth this admonition . . . But what mean these often admonitions and earnest exhortations of the Prophets, Apostles, Fathers, and holy doctors ?"—2 B. xi. 1.

52. "The holy Fathers, Job and Tobit."—*Ibid.*

53. "CHRIST, whose especial *favor* we may be assured by *this means to obtain*" [viz., by alms-giving].—2 B. xi. 2.

54. "Now will I . . . show unto you how *profita-*

ble it is for us to exercise them [alms-deeds] . . . [CHRIST'S saying] serveth to . . . prick us forwards . . . to learn . . . *how* we may *recover* our health, if it be lost or impaired, and how it may be defended and maintained if we have it. Yea, He teacheth us also therefore to esteem that as a *precious medicine* and an *inestimable jewel, that* hath such *strength and virtue* in it, that can either *procure* or preserve so incomparable a treasure."— *Ibid.*

55. "Then He and His disciples were grievously accused of the Pharisees, . . . because they went to meat and washed not their hands before, . . . CHRIST, answering their *superstitious* complaint, teacheth them an especial *remedy* how to *keep clean* their souls, . . . Give alms," &c.—*Ibid.*

56. "Merciful alms-dealing is *profitable* to *purge* the soul from the *infection and filthy spots of sin.*"—*Ibid.*

57. "The same lesson *doth the* HOLY GHOST *teach* in sundry places of the *Scripture*, saying, 'Mercifulness and alms-giving,' &c. [Tobit iv.] . . . The wise preacher, the son of Sirach, confirmeth the same, when he says, that 'as water quencheth burning fire,'" &c.—*Ibid.*

58. "A great *confidence* may they have *before the high* GOD, that show mercy and compassion to them that are afflicted."—*Ibid.*

59. "If ye have by any infirmity or weakness

been touched and annoyed with them . . . straight-way shall mercifulness *wipe and wash them away, as salves and remedies* to heal their *sores and grievous diseases.*"—*Ibid.*

60. "And therefore that *holy Father* Cyprian admonisheth to consider how *wholesome* and *profitable* it is to relieve the needy, &c. . . . . by *the which* we may *purge our sins* and *heal our wounded souls.*"—*Ibid.*

61. "We be therefore *washed* in our baptism from the *filthiness of sin*, that we should live afterwards in the pureness of life."—2 B. xiii. 1.

62. "By these means [by love, compassion, &c.] shall we *move* God to be *merciful to our sins.*"—*Ibid.*

63. "'He was dead,' saith St. Paul, 'for our sins, and rose again for our *justification*' . . . He died to destroy the rule of the devil in us, and He rose again to send down His HOLY SPIRIT *to rule in our hearts*, to endue us with *perfect righteousness.*"—2 B. xiv.

64. "The *ancient Catholic Fathers*," [in marg.] Irenæus, Ignatius, Dionysius, Origen, Optatus, Cyprian, Athanasius, . . . "were not afraid to call this supper, some of them, *the salve of immortality and sovereign preservative against death ;* other, the sweet dainties of our SAVIOUR, the pledge of eternal health, the defence of faith, the hope of the resurrection ; other, the *food of immor-*

6

tality, the healthful grace, and the conservatory to everlasting life."—2 B. xv. 1.

65. "The meat we seek in this supper is spiritual food, the nourishment of our soul, a heavenly refection, and not earthly; an *invisible meat*, and not bodily; a *ghostly substance*, and not carnal."—*Ibid*.

66. "Take this lesson . . . of Emissenus, a godly Father that . . . . thou *look up* with faith upon the *holy body and blood of thy* GOD, thou marvel with reverence, thou *touch* it with thy mind, thou receive it with the hand of thy heart, and thou take it fully with thy inward man."—*Ibid*.

67. "The saying of the holy martyr of GOD, St. Cyprian."—2 B. xx. 3.

Thus we see the authority of the Fathers, of the six first councils, and of the judgments of the Church generally, the holiness of the Primitive Church, the inspiration of the Apocrypha, the sacramental character of Marriage and other ordinances, the Real Presence in the Eucharist, the Church's power of excommunicating kings, the profitableness of fasting, the propitiatory virtue of good works, the Eucharistic commemoration, and justification by a righteousness [within us],* are taught in the Homilies. Let it be said again, it is not here asserted that a subscription to all and

---

* ·By inherent righteousness."—*First Edition*.

every of these quotations is involved in the subscription of an Article which does but generally
approve the Homilies; but they who insist so
strongly on our Church's holding that the Bishop
of Rome is Antichrist because the Homilies declare it, should recollect that there are other doctrines contained in them, beside it, which they
should be understood to hold, before their argument has the force of consistency.

§ 12.—*The Bishop of Rome.*

ARTICLE XXXVIII.—"The Bishop of Rome hath no jurisdiction in this realm of England."

By "hath" is meant "ought to have," as the Article in the 36th Canon and the Oath of Supremacy show, in which the same doctrine is drawn out more at length. "No foreign prince, person, *prelate*, state or potentate, hath, *or ought to have*, any jurisdiction, power, superiority, preeminence, or authority, ecclesiastical or spiritual, within this realm."

This is the profession which every one must in consistency make, who does not join the Roman Church. If the Bishop of Rome has jurisdiction and authority here, why do we not acknowledge it, and submit to him? To say then the above words, is nothing more or less than to say, "I am not a Roman Catholic;" and whatever reasons there are against saying them, are so far reasons against remaining in the English Church. They are a mere enunciation of the principle of Anglicanism.

Anglicans maintain that the supremacy of the

Pope is not directly from revelation, but an event in Providence. All things may be undone by the agents and causes by which they are done. What revelation gives, revelation takes away; what Providence gives, Providence takes away. GOD ordained by miracle, He reversed by miracle, the Jewish election; He promoted in the way of Providence, and He cast down by the same way, the Roman Empire. "The powers that be, are ordained of GOD," *while* they be, and have a claim on our obedience. When they cease to be, they cease to have a claim. They cease to be, when GOD removes them. He may be considered to remove them when He undoes what He had done. The Jewish election did not cease to be, when the Jews went into captivity: this was an event in Providence; and what miracle had ordained, it was miracle that annulled. But the Roman power ceased to be when the barbarians overthrew it; for it rose by the sword, and it therefore perished by the sword. The Gospel Ministry began in CHRIST and His Apostles: and what they began, they only can end. The Papacy began in the exertions and passions of man: and what man can make, man can destroy. Its jurisdiction, while it lasted, was " ordained of GOD;" when it ceased to be, it ceased to claim our obedience; and it ceased to be at the Reformation. The Reformers who could not destroy a Ministry, which the Apostles began, could destroy a Dominion which the Popes founded.

Perhaps the following passage will throw additional light upon this point :—

" The Anglican view of the Church has ever been this: that its portions need not otherwise have been united together for their essential completeness, than as being descended from one original. They are like a number of colonies sent out from a mother-country. . . Each Church is independent of all the rest, and is to act on the principle of what may be called Episcopal independence, except, indeed, so far as the civil power unites any number of them together. . . Each diocese is a perfect independent Church, sufficient for itself; and the communion of Christians one with another, and the unity of them altogether, lie, not in a mutual understanding, intercourse, and combination, not in what they do in common, but in what they are and have in common : in their possession of the Succession, their Episcopal form, their Apostolic faith, and the use of the Sacraments. . . Mutual intercourse is but an *accident* of the Church, not of its essence. . . Intercommunion is a duty, as other duties, but is not the tenure or instrument of the communion between the unseen world and this; and much more the confederacy of sees and churches, the metropolitan, patriarchal, and papal systems, are matters

of expedience or of natural duty from long custom,
or of propriety from gratitude and reverence, or
of necessity from voluntary oaths and engagements,
or of ecclesiastical force from the canons of Councils,
but not necessary in order to the conveyance of
grace, or for fulfilment of the ceremonial law, as
it may be called, of unity.   Bishop is superior to
bishop only in rank, not in real power; and the
Bishop of Rome, the head of the Catholic world,
is not the centre of unity, except as having a pri-
macy of order.   Accordingly, even granting, for
argument's sake, that the English Church violated
a duty in the 16th century, in releasing itself from
the Roman supremacy, still it did not thereby
commit that special sin, which cuts off from it the
fountains of grace, and is called schism.   It was
essentially complete without Rome, and naturally
independent of it; it had, in the course of years,
whether by usurpation or not, come under the
supremacy of Rome; and now, whether by rebellion
or not, it is free from it: and as it did not enter
into the Church invisible by joining Rome, so it
was not cast out of it by breaking from Rome.
These were accidents in its history, involving, indeed, sin in individuals, but not affecting the
Church as a Church.

" Accordingly, the Oath of Supremacy declares,
'that no foreign prelate hath, or ought to have,
any jurisdiction, power, pre-eminence, or authority

within this realm.'   In other words, there is noth_ing in the Apostolic system which gives an authority to the Pope over the Church, such as it does not give to a Bishop.   It is altogether an ecclesiastical arrangement; not a point *de fide*, but of expedience, custom, or piety, which cannot be claimed as if the Pope *ought* to have it, any more than, on the other hand, the King could of Divine right claim the supremacy; the claim of both one and the other resting, not on duty or revelation, but on specific engagement.   We find ourselves, as a Church, under the King now, and we obey him; we were under the Pope formerly, and we obeyed him.   'Ought' does not, in any degree, come into the question."

Conclusion.

ONE remark may be made in conclusion. It may be objected that the tenor of the above explanations is anti-Protestant, whereas it is notorious that the Articles were drawn up by Protestants, and intended for the establishment of Protestantism; accordingly, that it is an evasion of their meaning to give them any other than a Protestant drift, possible as it may be to do so grammatically, or in each separate part.

But the answer is simple:—

1. In the first place, it is a *duty* which we owe both to the Catholic Church and to our own, to take our reformed confessions in the most Catholic sense they will admit; we have no duties toward their framers. [Nor do we receive the Articles from their original framers, but from several successive convocations after their time; in the last instance, from that of 1662.]

2. In giving the Articles a Catholic interpretation, we bring them into harmony with the Book of Common Prayer, an object of the most serious moment in those who have given their assent to both formularies.

3. Whatever be the authority of the [Declaration] prefixed to the Articles, so far as it has any

6*

weight at all, it sanctions the mode of interpreting them above given. For its enjoining the
" literal and grammatical sense," relieves us from
the necessity of making the known opinions of
their framers, a comment upon their text ; and its
forbidding any person to " affix any *new* sense to
any Article," was promulgated at a time when
the leading men of our Church were especially
noted for those Catholic views which have been
here advocated.

4. It may be remarked, moreover, that such an
interpretation is in accordance with the well-
known general leaning of Melanchthon, from
whose writings our Articles are principally drawn,
and whose Catholic tendencies gained for him that
same reproach of popery, which has ever been so
freely bestowed upon members of our own reformed
Church.

"Melanchthon was of opinion," says Mosheim, "that, for the
sake of peace and concord, many things might be given up and
tolerated in the Church of Rome, which Luther considered could
by no means be endured . . In the class of matters indifferent,
this great man and his associates placed many things which had
appeared of the highest importance to Luther, and could not of
consequence be considered as indifferent by his true disciples
For he regarded as such, the doctrine of justification by faith
alone, the necessity of good works to eternal salvation, the
number of the sacraments, the jurisdiction claimed by the Pope
and the Bishops ; extreme unction, the observation of certain
religious festivals, and several superstitious rites and ceremonies."
—*Cent.* XVI., § 3, part 2, 27, 28.

5. Further; the Articles are evidently framed on the principle of leaving open large questions, on which the controversy hinges. They state broadly extreme truths, and are silent about their adjustment. For instance, they say that all necessary faith must be proved from Scripture, but do not say *who* is to prove it. They say that the Church has authority in controversies, they do not say *what* authority. They say that it may enforce nothing beyond Scripture, but do not say *where* the remedy lies when it does. They say that works *before* grace *and* justification are worthless and worse, and that works *after* grace and justification are acceptable, but they do not speak at all of works *with* GOD's aid, *before* justification. They say that men are lawfully called and sent to minister and preach, who are chosen and called by men who have public authority *given* them in the congregation to call and send; but they do not add *by whom* the authority is to be given. They say that councils called *by princes* may err; they do not determine whether councils called *in the name of* CHRIST will err.

[6. The variety of doctrinal views contained in the Homilies, as above shown, views which cannot be brought under Protestantism itself, in its greatest comprehension of opinions, is an additional proof, considering the connection of the Articles with the Homilies, that the Articles are not framed on

the principle of excluding those who prefer the
theology of the early ages to that of the Reformation; or rather let it be considered whether, considering both Homilies and Articles appeal to the
Fathers and Catholic antiquity, in interpreting
them by these, we are not going to the very authority to which they profess to submit themselves.]

7. Lastly, their framers constructed them in
such a way as best to comprehend those who did
not go so far in Protestantism as themselves.
Anglo-Catholics then are but the successors and
representatives of those moderate reformers; and
their case has been directly anticipated in the
wording of the Articles. It follows that they are
not perverting, they are using them, for an express
purpose for which among others their authors
framed them. The interpretation they take was
intended to be admissible; though not that which
their authors took themselves. Had it not been
provided for, possibly the Articles never would
have been accepted by our Church at all. If,
then, their framers have gained their side of the
compact in effecting the reception of the Articles,
let Catholics have theirs too in retaining their
own Catholic interpretation of them.

An illustration of this occurs in the history of
the 28th Article. In the beginning of Elizabeth's
reign a paragraph formed part of it, much like

that which is now appended to the Communion Service, but in which the Real Presence was *denied in words*. It was adopted by the clergy at the first convocation, but not published. Burnet observes on it thus:—

" When these Articles were at first prepared by the convocation in Queen Elizabeth's reign, this paragraph was made a part of them , for the original subscription by both houses of convocation, yet extant, shows this But the *design of the government* was at that time much turned *to the drawing over the body of the nation to the Reformation*, in whom the old leaven had gone deep, and no part of it deeper than the belief of the corporeal presence of CHRIST in the Sacrament , therefore it was *thought not expedient* to *offend* them by so particular a definition in this matter , in which the very word Real Presence was rejected It might, perhaps, be also suggested, that here a definition was made that went too much upon the principles of natural philosophy , which how true soever, they might not be the proper subject of an article of religion Therefore it was thought fit to suppress this paragraph ; though it was a part of the Article that was subscribed, yet it was not published, but the paragraph that follows, ' The Body of CHRIST,' &c , was put in its stead, and was received and published by the next convocation , which upon the matter was a full explanation of the way of CHRIST'S presence in this Sacrament , that 'He is present in a heavenly and spiritual manner, and that faith is the mean by which He is received ' This seemed to be more theological , and it does indeed amount to the same thing But howsoever we see what was the sense of the first convocation in Queen Elizabeth's reign , it differed in nothing from that in King Edward's time and therefore though this paragraph is now no part of our Articles, yet we are certain that the clergy at that time did not at all doubt of the truth of it ; we are sure it was their opinion , since they subscribed it, though *they did not think fit* to publish it at first ; and though it was afterwards changed for another, that was the same in sense "

What has lately taken place in the political world will afford an illustration in point. A French minister, desirous of war, nevertheless, as a matter of policy, draws up his state papers in such ' moderate language, that his successor, who is for peace, can act up to them, without compromising his own principles. The world, observing this, has considered it a circumstance for congratulation; as if the former minister, who acted a double part, had been caught in his own snare. It is neither decorous, nor necessary, nor altogether fair, to urge the parallel rigidly; but it will explain what is here meant to convey. The Protestant Confession was drawn up with the purpose of including Catholics; and Catholics now will not be excluded. What was an economy in the reformers, is a protection to us. What would have been a perplexity to us then, is a perplexity to Protestants now. We could not then have found fault with their words; they cannot now repudiate our meaning.

[J. H. N.]

OXFORD.
The Feast of the Conversion of St. Paul
1841.

SECOND EDITION.